PUPPETRY AND CREATIVE DRAMATICS
in storytelling

By Connie Champlin
Illustrated by Nancy Renfro

Puppetry in Education Series

A PUPPET CORNER IN EVERY LIBRARY

PUPPETRY AND THE ART OF STORY CREATION

PUPPETRY AND CREATIVE DRAMATICS IN STORYTELLING

Copyright © 1980 by Connie Champlin
all rights reserved
Published in the United States of America by
Nancy Renfro Studios   1117 W. 9th Street, Austin, Texas 78703
Library of Congress   PN1979.E4C47   372.6'4   80-15477
ISBN #0-931044-03-0

All photographs by Connie Champlin, Lauren Stockblower and Nancy Renfro

COVER CREDITS

front: Photo by Lauren Stockblower
Matthew Teeter, Michael Yukica and Ander Longenderfer
Central Baptist Nursery School

back: Photo by Connie Champlin
Laura Price with plastic bottle puppet
Puppet idea by Frank Wickham, 6th grade teacher
Laura Dodge Elementary School, Omaha, NE

For Jack
who believed

THE CHILDREN:

Laura Price
Danny Potter
Gina Weberg
Jason Wynn
Angela Newnham
Nora Rashid
Kathleen Traurig
Brian Whittenbrook
Staci Davis
Bradley Kuhn
Kimberly Carlisle
Savannah Gorell
Eric Pumphret
Paul Briggs
Sarah Turman
Brett Goss

Kevin Ascherfield
Monica Arellani
Robin Foye
Daniel Cassles
Robert Torres
Paula Meyer
Matthew Teeter
Michael Yukica
Ander Longenderfer
Emily Powell
Rebecca Dohner
Kerry Francis
Timothy Schrodel
Maria Angelo
Terry Naraine
Garwell Harrison
Kylon Rolles
Carrie Wais
Brian Yauger

THE SCHOOLS:

Mason Elementary School—Omaha, NE
Laura Dodge Elementary School—Omaha, NE
Edison Elementary School—Omaha, NE
Mommouth Park Elementary School—Omaha, NE
Clifton Hill Elementary School—Omaha, NE
Rosehill Elementary School—Omaha, NE
Dundee Elementary School—Ohama, NE
Cunningham Elementary School—Austin, TX
Texas State School for the Deaf—Austin, TX
Cedar Creek Elementary School —Austin, TX
Belmont Street Community School — Worcester, MA
Mercer Crest Elementary School — Mercer Island, WA
Central Baptist Nursery School—Wayne, PA

ACKNOWLEDGEMENTS

The ideas for this book developed from my master's thesis in drama. Many people have contributed to its final shape. My sincere thanks to:

The children of Belmont Street Community School in Worcester, Massachusetts, and Mercer Crest Elementary School in Mercer Island, Washington who participated in my learning.

Nancy Renfro for her friendship and support of my work.

Agnes Haaga, my thesis advisor at the University of Washington, for her suggestions.

Dr. Fred Anderson, Director of Media Services, Omaha Public Schools for the opportunity to experiment and develop new projects.

Teachers, librarians, and children of the Omaha Public Schools for sharing their creativity with me, especially Carol Anderson, Art Supervisor, Mary Heise and Barb Kennedy, Librarians.

Ann Weiss Schwalb, Children's Librarian, Tredyffrin Public Library of Strafford, Pennsylvania, who serves as chief editor and consultant for this *Pupperty in Education book series.*

The children of: Cunningham Elementary School, Austin, Texas, and instructor Carmen Di Nino; Central Baptist Nursery School, Wayne, Pennsylvania, and director Carol Tatta; and Zachary Scott Theater, Austin, Texas, and creative dramatics teacher, Alice Wilson, for allowing us to photograph storytelling in action.

Puppeteers of America and *The Puppetry in Education* organizations for expanding my knowledge and broadening my perspective of puppetry.

TABLE OF CONTENTS

INTRODUCTION

Children grow and learn through play. Dramatic play, in which a child "becomes" a part of a story, stimulates the imagination, develops language, and gives children great delight.

Imagine a child's excitement in creating voices for puppet characters from folklore. Images painted in a poem are sharpened in the eye of the mind, as a child interprets them through pantomime. Creating sounds and actions for a story involves a child in three broad avenues of experience: physical, emotional, and intellectual. Combining drama with children, good literature, and an enthusiastic leader results in an exciting literature program.

Some of the ideas described in this book can be incorporated into the story as you are telling it; others might be more appropriate to do after the story is told. The concept is to involve you and the students into drama slowly, with exercises that build on one another. The beginning activities involve imagining and making sound effects within the security of a group situation. Gradually those activities requiring more individual participation are introduced.

If you have not been using drama you may wish to do the activities as sequenced. However, if participation is not new to you and the children, you may decide to select and do activities according to your own interests.

As you begin, keep in mind these two keys to success—be well prepared and enjoy yourself.

HOW TO BEGIN

Rather than making it an entirely new activity, incorporate drama into your existing program. Use of storytelling techniques and finger plays are standard in most library programs; the next time you share a story, ask the children to help by contributing the sound effects (from objects and instruments found in your sound effects resource box.) Or you might set up a "Costume Corner" with samples of hats, scarves, and other finery which children can use to become characters from a story. You've begun to use drama.

—BE CONFIDENT. The children are going to enjoy being involved. Use a physical environment in which you feel most comfortable. Select stories, poems and activities you completely enjoy; attitudes and feelings are readily discerned by the audience and, in fact, are often mirrored by the children. Practice reading or telling the story before actually doing it with your audience. You might wish to begin with a small group the first time you do an activity.

—EXPLAIN THE ACTIVITY CLEARLY AND CONCISELY TO THE CHILDREN. Help them focus their concentration by asking key questions. Be sure all the children understand what they are going to do before you begin.

—BEGIN WITH STRUCTURE. This is particularly true when dramatic involvement is new to the children. They may not know how to respond to this new type of freedom and responsibility. You and the children will feel more comfortable working within a limited space at the beginning. It is easier to allow the children more space and greater participation when they are ready for it, than it is to restrict them once they have begun.

—BUILD IN A CONTROL FACTOR AT THE BEGINNING OF EACH ACTIVITY. You might use a simple clap of your hands, a word signal, or drum beat at which everyone freezes. If children become overexcited you can immediately have them freeze. Then you may either give a new direction or discuss what is happening, and then continue.

If one child begins to bother others, speak to him/her about unacceptable behavior. If the disruptive behavior continues, ask the child to leave the group.

—USE YOUR VOICE OR MUSIC TO CREATE AN ATMOSPHERE. This will help the children become involved.

—BEGIN WITH GROUP ACTIVITIES IN WHICH ALL THE CHILDREN PARTICIPATE SIMULTANEOUSLY. Later, you may wish to have children working in pairs and then in small groups. Children should not "act" in front of others until they are ready and willing to do so.

—NEVER FORCE A CHILD TO PARTICIPATE: Some children may be reluctant at first; let them be non-participating members of the group until they are ready to join in the activity. On the other hand, do not allow a child who is not involved to spoil the activity for others through disruptive behavior.

Before beginning an activity, tell the children if they do not wish to participate, they may sit apart from the group and watch quietly.

—DO DRAMA IN YOUR OWN WAY. Adapt activities in accordance with your own ideas and experiences.

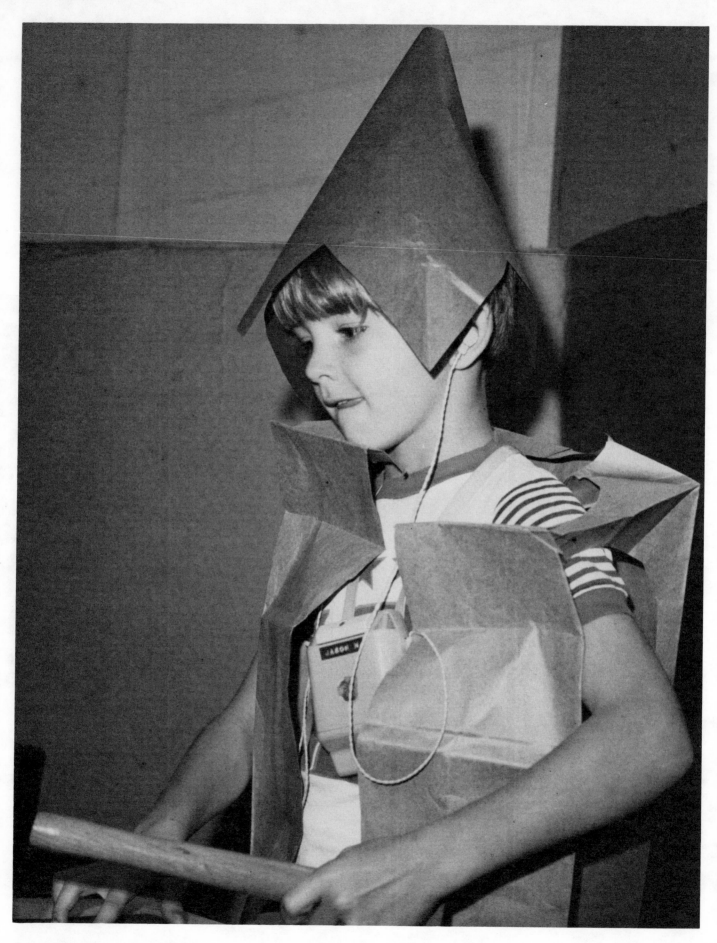

A simple paper bag costume.

IMAGINATION

DRAMATIC ACTIVITY: Using a prop to stimulate imagination.

LITERATURE: Grimm, Jacob and Wilhelm. *The Elves and the Shoemaker*.

TO THE LEADER: An object related to a story can be used to stimulate a child's imagination. For example, a shoe has an apparent and well-known function in "The Elves and the Shoemaker." The shoe in this story is central to the plot. Using this object as a focal point, develop experiences and key questions which encourage children to stretch their imagination.

PREPARATION: Collect several types of shoes, for example, a heavy boot, high heel, ballet slipper, Indian moccasin.

Display books about elves and versions of "The Elves and the Shoemaker."

INTRODUCTION: "How many different kinds of shoes can you name?"

Hold up a shoe. "How would you walk if you were wearing a pair of shoes like this one?" If the space is too small for all to move at once, show shoe to a small group and have them "walk" for the class. Ask class to name type of shoe being worn. Repeat activity with several types of shoes, allowing a different group to "walk" each time.

PRESENTATION: "Who makes shoes?" Discuss how shoes are made. With group sitting, pantomime together the processes involved in making shoes; cutting leather, sewing pieces together, hammering, etc.

"What do you think an elf looks like?" Accept all ideas. "Listen as I tell the story of 'The Elves and the Shoemaker' and imagine what the characters look like."

Tell the story. After the story, let the children discuss why the elves helped the shoemaker.

Invite children to draw their interpretation of the elves or the shoemaker. Share their illustrations and then examine illustrations of elves from books. Stress that there is no one way of portraying a character.

FOLLOW-UP:

1. Versions of "The Elves and the Shoemaker:"

   Grimm, Jacob and Wilhelm. *The Shoemaker and the Elves.* Illus. by Ardienne Adams. Charles Scribner's Sons, 1960.·
   _____. *The Fairy Tale Treasury.* Edited by Virginia Haviland. Coward, McCann and Geoghegan, 1972, Pp. 118–21.
   Littledale, Freya. *The Elves and the Shoemaker.* Four Winds, 1975.

2. Display other books about elves.

   Adshead, Gladys L. *Brownies—Hush!* H. Z. Walck, 1938. A modern version of "The Elves and the Shoemaker."
   Belting, Natalia. *Elves and Ellefolk.* Holt, Rinehart and Winston, 1961.
   Lindgren, Astrid. *The Tomten.* Adapted by Astrid Lindgren from a poem by Viktor Rydberg. Coward McCann, 1961.
   Palmer, Robin and Doane, Pelagie. *Fairy Elves.* H. Z. Walck, 1964.

VARIATIONS:

1. Create a puppet from a found object.

2. Introduce other stories using objects to stimulate imagination.

a. Box

Ask children, "What do you think is in this box?" Children may either tell what they think, or open the box and show what they think is in it. After the story give them an opportunity to react to the box as it was represented in the story.

   Benson, Sally. "Pandora, the First Woman." In Sally Benson, *Stories of the Gods and Heroes.* Dial Press, 1940. Pp. 29–34.
   Rudolph, Marguarita. *I Am Your Misfortune.* Seabury Press, 1968.
   Craig, Jean. *A Dragon in the Clock Box.* Norton, 1962.

b. Stone

   Baylor, Byrd. *Everybody Needs a Rock.* Scribner, 1974.

Brown, Marcia. *Stone Soup*. Scribner, 1947.
Crampton, Anne Eliot. *The Lifting Stone*. Holiday, 1978.
Seskin, Stephen. *Stone in the Road*. Van Nostrand, 1968.

c. Clock

Bellairs, John. *House With a Clock in Its Walls*. Dial Press, 1973.
Hutchins, Pat. *Clocks and More Clocks*. MacMillan, 1970.

d. Bag

Balian, Lorna. *The Aminal*. Abingdon, 1972.

3. Display a variety of unusual props, such as an ostrich feather, worn top hat, rusty key. Individually or in small groups encourage children to develop a story around the prop. Stories can then be dramatized, written and/or illustrated.

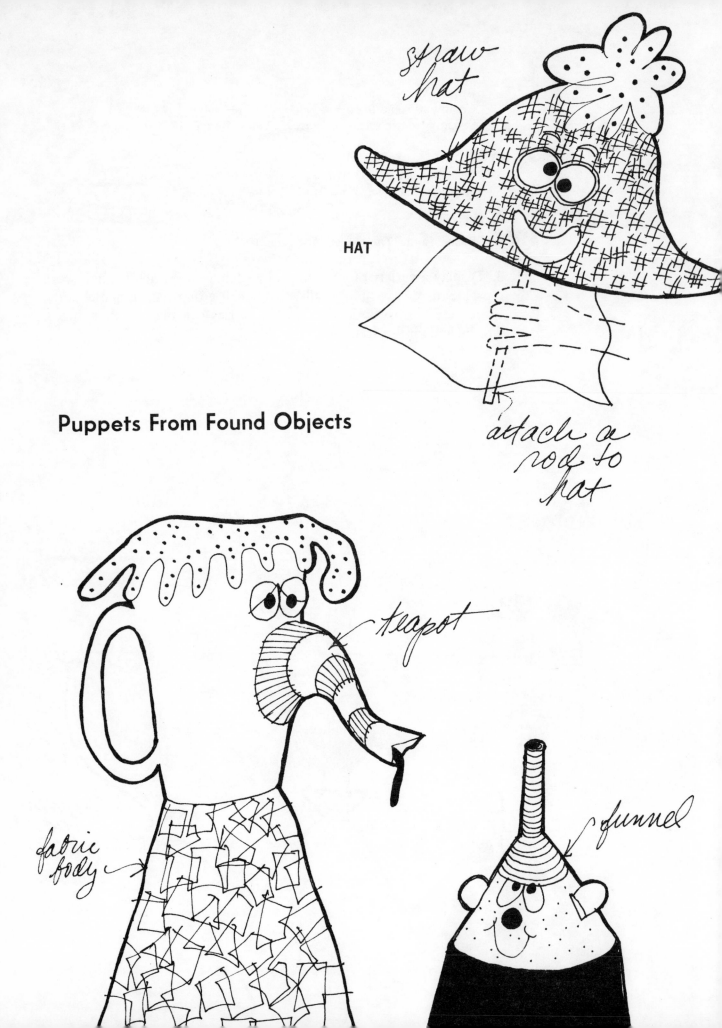

straw
hat

HAT

attach a
rod to
hat

Puppets From Found Objects

teapot

funnel

fabric
body

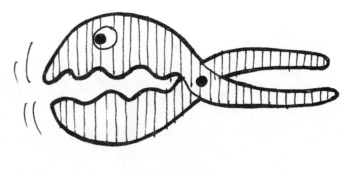

PLIERS

KITCHEN UTENSILS

Spatula

feather duster

wooden spoon rubber band and cloth body

A BROOM PUPPET

This presentation of The Shoemaker and The Elves by older students
is narrated completely from a newspaper, by a reporter.

DIALOGUE

DRAMATIC ACTIVITY: Expressing mood and feeling through dialogue.

LITERATURE: Sendak, Maurice. *Pierre*. Harper & Row, 1962.

TO THE LEADER: Stories, such as *Pierre,* which contain a response repeated by one or more characters, provide an opportunity for children to express meaning and feeling through their voices. When students say "I don't care" as Pierre, they are using only their voice to communicate characterization. Each child decides for him/herself what a character is like. The child must then decide how to express with his/her voice the character's opinion of the remarks made by other characters in the story. Allow each child to discover his/her own way to interpret and respond to the situations presented in the story.

INTRODUCTION: Write a sentence such as "I don't want to play with you" on the board. Ask a child to say the sentence.

"Can anyone say this sentence in a different way?" Encourage children to find as many varied ways of saying this same sentence as possible. Help the children to discover that by putting emphasis on different words new meanings are created.

PRESENTATION: "I'd like you to help me tell a story about a boy named Pierre. Throughout this story, Pierre replies. "I don't care" to everything that anyone says to him. He says "I don't care" once too often and something dreadful happens. When I point to you during the story, say 'I don't care' as if you are Pierre."

Tell the story pointing to individual children to supply the dialogue.

FOLLOW-UP:

1. Present stories about characters who *do* care and cooperate.

Delton, Judy. *Two Good Friends*. Crown, 1974.

Grimm, Jacob and Wilhelm. *The Bremen Town Musicians*. Illus. by Paul Galdone. McGraw Hill, 1968.

Holmes, Efner Tudor. *Carrie's Gift*. Collins-World, 1978.

Marshall, James. *What's the Matter With Carruthers?* Houghton, 1972.

2. Read some poems about other children who didn't care. Compare their fate to Pierre's.

Hoffman, Heinrich. "The Story of Augustus Who Would Not Have Any Soup." In William Cole (Comp.), *Beastly Boys and Ghastly Girls*. World, 1964. Pp. 48–9.

Rands, William Brightly. "Godfrey Gordon Gustuvus Gore." In William Cole (Comp.), *Oh, That's Ridiculous*. Viking, 1972. Pp. 42–3.

Silverstein, Shel. "Sarah Cynthia Sylvia Stout Would Not Take the Garbage Out." In Shel Silverstein, *Where the Sidewalk Ends*. Harper & Row, 1974.

VARIATIONS:

1. Other stories to use for creating dialogue include:

Carle, Eric. *Have You Seen My Cat?* Watts, 1973.

Galdone, Paul. *The Little Red Hen*. Seabury, 1973.

Leister, Mary. *The Silent Concert*. Bobbs Merrill, 1970.

Mendoza, George. "The Devil's Pocket." In George Mendoza, *The Crack in the Wall and Other Terribly Weird Tales*. Dial Press, 1967. Pp. 5–15.

Poulshkin, Maria. *Mother, Mother I Want Another*. Crown, 1978.

Richter, Mischa. *Quack?* Harper, 1978.

Use paper envelope puppets to characterize dialogue.

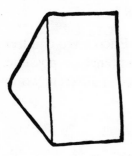

1. Paper envelope.

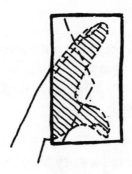

2. Tuck flap of envelope inside. Place hand inside as shown.

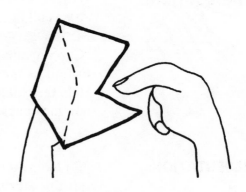

3. Gently "bite" finger of other hand to form mouth. Straighten out mouth if wrinkled.

To the basic head add ears, jaws, a funny nose or a trunk for an elephant; bend back the tips to make a snout for a pig.

For extra strength, use two envelopes, doubled up. Envelopes may be painted, but allow to dry well before using. Also, use better quality envelopes because cheap quality ones tend to fall apart when painted.

Paper-Envelope Puppets
VARIATION

Using paper envelope puppets to characterize dialogue

add paper nose

yarn or paper hair

glue on fabric costume over paper body cutout.

PIERRE

paper fringe

pom pom nose

LION

paper body

27

CONFLICT

DRAMATIC ACTIVITY: Using voice to express conflict.

LITERATURE: Gag, Wanda. *Millions of Cats*. Coward-McCann, 1928.

TO THE LEADER :   *Millions of Cats* is a picture book written in folktale style. It is the story of a lonely old man and woman who want a cat. The rhythmic refrain repeated throughout the story heightens the old man's problem. He cannot decide which cat to choose so he brings home "hundreds of cats, thousands of cats, millions and billions and trillions of cats."

The children participate in the story's conflict and its resolution by chanting the refrain and becoming the voices of the fighting cats.

PREPARATION: Print the refrain on a posterboard:

> *Hundreds of cats,*
> *Thousands of cats,*
> *Millions and billions and trillions of cats.*

Arrange book display.

INTRODUCTION: "Have you ever seen a million of anything?"

Develop the idea that a million is an extremely large amount—blades of grass, grains of sand. This will aid the children in enjoying the humor of the story.

"Today I'm going to tell a story about millions of cats. I need your help."

PRESENTATION: "There's a section of the story that is repeated over and over, like a chorus in a song. In a story the chorus is called a refrain. Listen while I say the refrain for our story: 'Hundreds of cats, thousands of cats, millions and billions and trillions of cats.' "

Have the children practice saying the refrain several times. Display the poster where it can be seen.

"There's a part in the story where the cats have a terrible argument. What sounds do angry cats make?" Allow children time to respond.

"When I hold up my hand closed in a fist like this (demonstrate) it will be your signal to get ready to make fight sounds. When I begin to open my fist, you start quietly to make cat sounds. The more I open my fist, the louder your sounds should become. When my hand is open the fight should be at its peak. As I begin to close my hand, make your sounds become quieter and quieter. When my fist is closed again, there should be no sound at all. Let's try it. Remember to keep your eyes on my fist."

Practice several times until the children can regulate volume according to your hand signal.

Tell the story with or without the book. Encourage children's participation with voice and eye cues.

FOLLOW-UP: 1. Introduce other books by Wanda Gag:

—*ABC Bunny*. Coward, 1933.
—*Funny Thing*. Coward, 1929.
—*Nothing at All*. Coward, 1941.
—*Jorinda and Joringel*. Coward, McCann & Geoghegan, 1978.

2. Display books about real cats.

Burger, Carl. *All About Cats*. Random House, 1966.
Selsam, Millicent E. *How Kittens Grow*. Four Winds, 1975.
Ylla. *I'll Show You Cats*. Harper & Row, 1964.

VARIATIONS: 1. Tell the story using paper strip puppets or paper plate masks.

2. Tell the story *Millions of Cats* again with the children using rhythm instruments in addition to their voices to show the conflict.

3. Tell the story "The Fisherman and His Wife" in this manner. The

conflict in this story is seen in the changing form of the sea. One group can chant the refrain:

> Flounder, flounder in the sea,
> Prithee harken unto me,
> Ilsebil, my willful wife,
> Does not want my way of life.

Another group may use rhythm instruments to make the sounds of the sea. A third group uses its voice to create the changing sounds of the wind. The intensity and volume of the sounds will show the growing story conflict.

Versions of "The Fisherman and His Wife" include:

Grimm, Jacob and Wilhelm. *The Fisherman and His Wife*. Illus. by Madeleine Gekieve. Pantheon, 1957.

————. *The Fisherman and His Wife*. By Harve and Margot Zemach. Norton, 1966.

————. *Grimm's Fairy Tales*. Follett, 1968. Pp. 78–81.

————. *Tales From Grimm*. Translated and illus. by Wanda Gag. Coward, 1936. Pp. 149–68.

rubber cement paper claws on fingers→

cut out eyeholes

tie string to holes in sides of plates

paper-plate

Paper-Plate Masks

Glue on sequin eyes, yarn whiskers, button noses, etc.

MILLIONS OF CATS

Cotton hair

OLD WOMAN

OLD MAN

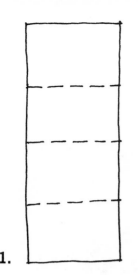

1.

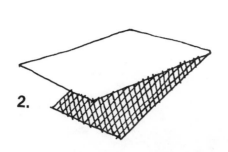

2.

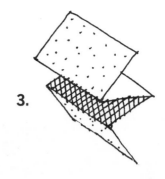

3.

Paper-Strip Puppets

1. Cut a strip of construction paper 4" x 12".
2. Fold in half.
3. Fold in quarters.
4. Open out ends and create a simple face on front flap section. Operate puppet from back as shown.

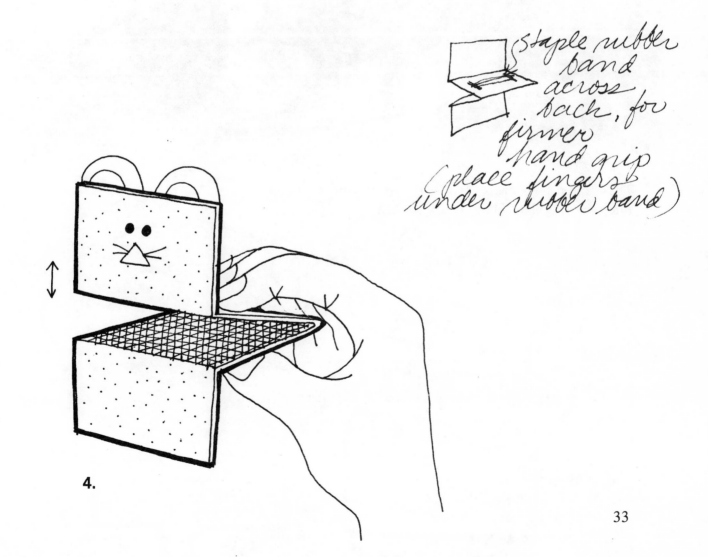

staple rubber band across back, for firmer hand grip (place fingers under rubber band)

4.

These three boys are shown in a free playing situation,
interpretating The Three Bears to their own style.

STORYTELLING WITH FREE STANDING PUPPETS

DRAMATIC ACTIVITY: Creating dialogue with puppets.

LITERATURE: *The Story of the Three Bears*, a traditional story.

TO THE LEADER : The stories described in this section are similar. Each has a single theme, uncomplicated plot, and is familiar to the children. The dialogue is simple and moves the action of the story forward. The dialogue matches the action of the characters; it is the action spoken.

By providing the voices of characters, children are able to live the story more completely. Because the whole group responds together, the less secure child will not feel threatened. The children remain in their seats while participating in this dramatic experience.

PREPARATION: Make the puppets. The puppets are designed to stand independently allowing you to use more than two puppets at a time. (Instructions follow.)

Practice telling the story using the puppets and supplying all the dialogue yourself.

Since the children will be asked to supply the dialogue during the storytelling, be sure they are familiar with the story.

PHYSICAL SETTING: Manipulate the puppets on a low bookcase or table as you tell the story. Children sit on the floor in front of you.

INTRODUCTION: As children enter the library their interest will be aroused by seeing

Mama, Papa, and Baby Bear puppet in place on top of a table or book-case. Make sure Goldilocks is out of sight but close at hand.

Ask the children if they know what story will be told. Ask if there are any other characters in the story. Bring Goldilocks forward. "Why is she called Goldilocks?"

PRESENTATION: Discuss the setting for the story.

"Where does the story take place?"
Describe the forest, pointing out a tall pine tree, a tiny mushroom, a babbling brook, etc. Have children close their eyes and imagine what the forest looks like and what sounds they would hear.

"Where do the Three Bears live? How many rooms are needed in this story?"
Show with your hands which section of the table will be the kitchen, living room, bedroom. Ask the children to imagine what the house and its furnishings look like.

Discuss the characters in the story.

Introduce each puppet and invite the children to say "Good Morning" as if they were the character.
Review incidents in the story and ask how each character feels and responds, such as:

"How does Baby Bear feel when he sees his broken chair? What does he say?"
"How does Papa Bear sound when he becomes angry?"
"How does Goldilocks sound when she tastes Mama Bear's Porridge?"

Practice some of the dialogue in the story with the children providing the character voices as you move individual puppets. Encourage children to use appropriate emotions and vocal timbre for each character. If children use an extremely high, screechy voice for Baby Bear or over-exaggerate the voices of the other characters, discuss more appropriate voice characterizations. Children should strive for a genuine image.

Discuss sound effects in the story.

"What sound effects are needed in this story?" (chair breaking, knocking on door, forest sounds)
Ask children to make the sound effects. Encourage each child to respond in his own way.

Narrate the story using the puppets. Leave Goldilocks out of sight until needed. When the bears go for a walk they can stand in view in an area that has been designated as the forest.

36

Cue children to their participation with lead lines such as:

—"Goldilocks tasted Mama Bear's porridge and said, (pause for children to provide dialogue)."

—"Papa Bear scowled when he saw his chair and said in an angry voice, (pause)."

—"When Baby Bear looked at his broken chair he said in a small voice filled with tears, (pause)."

If children do not respond, you provide the dialogue and continue with the story. The first time you do this type of activity, the children may seem uncertain and timid. Give them time and encouragement, and they will begin to respond eagerly.

FOLLOW-UP:

1. Present books containing various versions of *"The Three Bears."* Discuss the reason for variations in folklore.

Brokke, L. Leslie. *The Golden Goose Book.* Frederick Warne, n.d., n.p.
Great Children's Stories: The *Classic Volland Edition.* Hubbard Press, 1972. Pp. 27–35.
Haviland, Virginia. *The Fairy Tale Treasury.* Coward, McCann and Geoghegan, 1972. Pp. 36–43.
The Tall Book of Nursery Tales. Illus. by Feodor Rojankovsky. Harper, 1944. Pp. 377–45.
Rockwell, Anne. *The Three Bears & 15 Other Stories.* Crowell, 1976.

2. Display other nursery tales.

Asbjornsen, P. C. *The Three Billy Goats Gruff.* Illus. by Marcia Brown. Harcourt, Brace and World, 1957.
De Regniers, Beatrice Schenk. *Red Riding Hood.* Atheneum, 1972.
Galdone, Paul. *The Gingerbread Boy.* Seabury, 1975.
The Three Little Pigs. Illus. by William Pene Du Bois. Viking, 1972.

3. Introduce a variety of books about bears, real and fictional.

FICTIONAL BEARS

Asch, Frank. *Moon Bear.* Scribner, 1978.
Minarik, Else. *Little Bear.* Harper, 1957.
Steiner, Jorg. *Bear Who Wanted to Be a Bear.* Atheneum, 1977.
Turkle, Brinton. *Deep in the Forest.* Dutton, 1976.

REAL BEARS

Eberle, Irmengarde. *Bears Live Here.* Doubleday, 1966.
Grosveno, Donna. *Pandas.* National Geographic Society, 1973.
Naden, Corinne. *Let's Find Out About Bears.* Watts, 1971.

4. Leave the puppets on a table so children can informally recreate the story themselves or for others.

VARIATIONS:

1. Have the children pantomime the story as it is narrated. Use simple costume suggestions and real props, if desired.

2. Divide the class into four groups. Each group does the voice for a specific character.

3. Do the story several times using a different version each time.

ADDITIONAL STORIES:

The following stories can all be done using the same physical arrangement, puppet style, and presentation format as "The Three Bears." If you want to try other stories, be sure to select those in which the dialogue is the action spoken.

1. "The Three Billy Goats Gruff"

Children can create voices of the goats and the troll as well as the hoof sounds on the bridge. The goat puppets can be made in the same free standing style as the bear puppets. A cereal or potato chip box can be used as the base for the Troll. Paint the box green and use fake fur, yarn, felt, and paint for features and hair.

2. "The Three Little Pigs"

Children can create voices for the pigs and the wolf as well as a variety of sound effects. A chimney and soup pot made from tag board will add to the fun of this story. Puppets can all be constructed in the free standing style.

3. "Henny Penny"

Children can make all the animal sounds as well as asking Henny Penny where she is going and if they may accompany her. The first time this story is done, you should be Henny Penny and the Fox since their dialogue is more involved. Children can take over these roles as well after several playings.

Puppets can all be constructed in the free standing style.

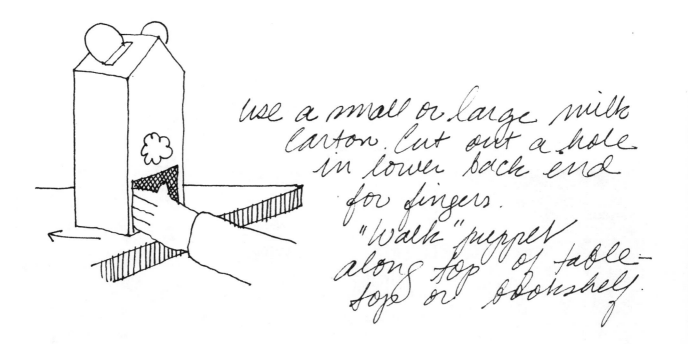

use a small or large milk carton. Cut out a hole in lower back end for fingers.

"Walk" puppet along top of table-tops or bookshelf.

Free-Standing Puppets

simple stand-up scenery constructed from grocery carton cardboard can be fun to try!

STAND-UP SCENERY

cotton ball, button or pom pom noses

curly paper hair

THE THREE BEARS

GOLDILOCKS

Goldilocks is characterized by a wig, while the Three Bears wear varied hats (baby bonnet, woman's and man's hat), and fur collars.

They are following up the puppet activity with an improvisational pantomime sketch, sequencing the entire story. Note the simple use of props, such as: two rugs and a doll's bed, for the beds; three varied size chairs; and assorted plastic bowls on a table.

SOUND EFFECTS

DRAMATIC ACTIVITY:

Creating atmosphere with sounds to express the mood of a story.

LITERATURE:

Mendoza, George. *The Hairy Toe*. In George Mendoza, *Gwot!*. Harper & Row, 1967. P. 19–27.

TO THE LEADER :

"*The Hairy Toe*" is a ghost story about a creature searching for its hairy toe, which has been swallowed by an old hag. A repetitious chant adds to the suspense of this story

Invite the group to help you tell this story by creating an eerie, suspenseful atmosphere. Individual children may be responsible for specific sounds. The remainder of the group may create the voice crying for its hairy toe.

Encourage children to join with you in the storytelling but do not force them to participate. Sitting together in a familiar storytelling setting creates a secure, sharing environment. This creativity is a beginning step towards increased dramatic involvement.

PREPARATION:

Collect and experiment with a variety of rhythm instruments including:

  —sand blocks
  —castanets
  —rhythm sticks
  —drums
  —wooden blocks
  —guiro

If rhythm instruments are not available, any collection of sound makers can be used; coffee can drums, sticks, containers filled with rice, sand, stones, etc.

45

Practice telling the story.

Arrange book display.

PHYSICAL SETTING: Children sit on floor in the storytelling area. Dim the lights. If told on Halloween, a Jack-o-lantern with a burning candle will help create an atmosphere.

INTRODUCTION: Have children close their eyes and imagine an old, crooked, deserted house on a windy night. Discuss sounds which they are apt to hear.

"The Hairy Toe" is a ghost story which takes place in the house of an old hag at midnight. I want you to help me make the sound effects."

PRESENTATION: Bring out the instruments and demonstrate their use. Ask children which instrument should be used to make the sound effects needed; running, locking door and shutters, stirring, snoring, croaking, wind coiling and wailing, boards creaking, shutters rapping, chimney rumbling, door opening, house shaking. Children may decide to use their voices for some of the sound effects.

Select children to play each instrument. Allow each a chance to make the needed sound effect as the rest of the group listens. Encourage suggestions for alternate ways of producing a similar effect.

Those children not making a specific sound will repeat the creature's chant, "Who's got my hairy toe?"

Tell the story pausing for the sound effects.

FOLLOW-UP: 1. What kind of creature has lost its hairy toe? What does it look like? Ask children to draw or pantomime their version of the creature.

2. Introduce other ghost stories.

Chase, Richard. "*Wicked John and the Devil.*" In Richard Chase. *Grandfather Tales*. Houghton Mifflin, 1948. Pp. 29–39.
Galdone, Paul. *The Tailypo*. Seabury Press, 1977.
Wickes, Frances. "*Wait Till Martin Comes.*" In Wilhelmina Harper (Ed.), *Ghosts and Goblins*. Dutton, 1965. Pp. 194–196.

3. Display collections of ghost or supernatural stories.

Harter, Walter. *Osceola's Head & Other American Ghost Stories*. Prentice-Hall, 1974.

Ireson, Barbara. *Haunting Tales*. Dutton, 1974.

Leach, Marcia. *Whistle in the Graveyard*. Viking, 1974.

Prelutsky, Jack. *Nightmares: Poems to Trouble Your Sleep*. Greenwillow, 1976.

VARIATIONS:

1. Use paper plate puppets to tell the story.

2. Tell the story of *"The Hairy Toe"* using voice and body sounds (clapping, slapping floor) in lieu of instruments to create sound effects.

Ask children to sit in a circle. Then ask everyone to think of a sound they might hear on a dark, windy night as they approached a haunted house. Point to a child who makes a sound. Everyone listens and then echoes that sound. When a sound is needed in the story, everyone makes the sound in their own way.

3. Create sound effects for stories involving other environments, such as the sea, the jungle, or the city.

4. Using a cumulative story such as, "The Old Woman and Her Pig," create a musical sound for each character in the story. Whenever that character is mentioned the corresponding sound is made.

Stories which can be done in this manner include:

Aardema, Verna. *Why Mosquitoes Buzz in People's Ears*. Dial, 1975.

Burningham, John. *Mr. Gumpy's Outing*. Holt, Rinehart & Winston, 1970.

Emberley, Barbana. *Drummer Hoff*. Prentice Hall, 1967.

Galdone, Paul. *Little Tuppen*. Seabury, 1967.

Jameson, Cynthia. *The Clay Pot Boy*. Coward, McCann & Geoghegan, 1973.

Wahl, Jan. *Drakestail*. Greenwillow, 1978.

Paper-Plate Puppets

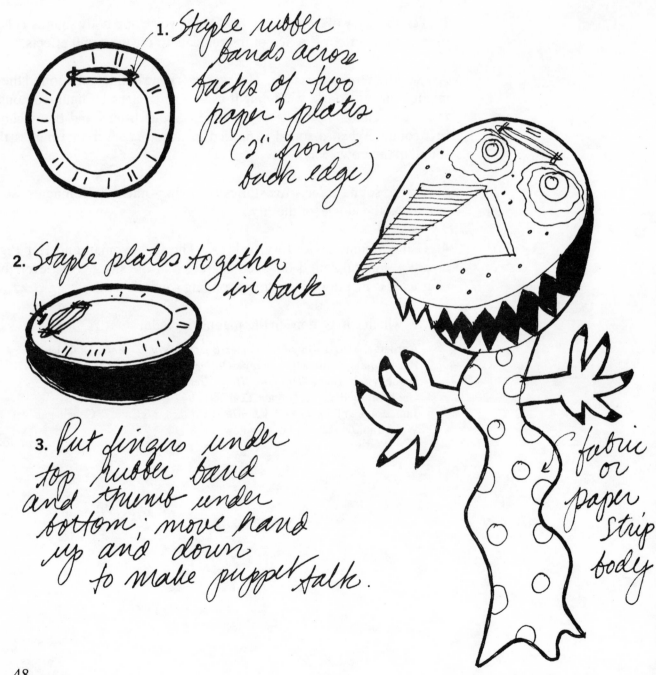

1. Staple rubber bands across backs of two paper plates (2" from back edge)

2. Staple plates together in back

3. Put fingers under top rubber band and thumb under bottom; move hand up and down to make puppet talk.

fabric or paper strip body

48

SCAREY CREATURE

paper fringe hair

*paper envelope puppet
(see page 27)*

OLD HAG

paper cutout body

49

CARDBOARD ROD PUPPETS

1. Cut out large shapes from poster board or other stiff cardboard to represent characters.
2. Decorate shapes with paint, scrap fabric, yarn, cotton, buttons and other odds and ends.
3. Secure shapes to stick or rod handles.

STORYTELLING WITH ROD PUPPETS

DRAMATIC ACTIVITY:

Correlating puppet actions and sounds to create a story.

LITERATURE:

McGovern, Ann. *Too Much Noise*. Houghton Mifflin, 1967.

TO THE LEADER:

Too Much Noise is a humorous story about a man so annoyed by ordinary household sounds that he seeks the advice of a wise man. The farmer follows the wise man's counsel and brings the farm animals into the house. The farmer's realization of how quiet his house actually was comes only after the animals have been removed.

This picture book presents a new twist to the popular folktale about a house which seems too crowded.

Too Much Noise presents many opportunities for children to create sounds, rhythms, and movements for puppet characters. Children may chose to participate by manipulating the puppets, creating animal rhythms and other sound effects.

PREPARATION:

Make puppets of a cow, donkey, sheep, hen, dog, cat, wise man, the farmer Peter.

Practice telling the story.

Assemble a variety of materials which can be used for creating sounds:

>—rhythm and toy instruments
>—sand paper blocks
>—rice in tin can
>—tissue paper

Define an area for the house. This could be as simple as two desks, bookcases, chairs, or even tape on the floor.

PHYSICAL SETTING:

Designate an area for the wise man's house and another for Peter's house. The area for the barnyard should be far enough away to give the puppeteers a chance to move freely as the animal characters. All the children making sound effects can sit on the floor in a fourth area.

Sample arrangement:

Sound Effects Section

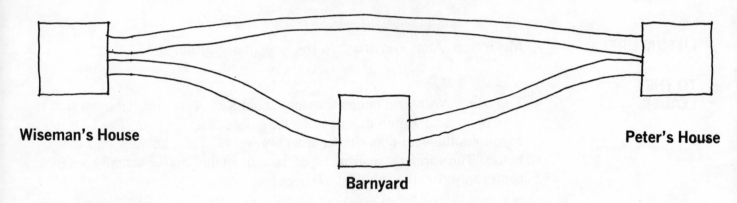

Wiseman's House

Barnyard

Peter's House

INTRODUCTION:

"Close your eyes and listen to all the sounds in this room. (Pause) Now listen for all the sounds outside the room. As you listen imagine who or what is making the sound." (Pause)

List all the sounds heard. "Were any of the sounds unusual, sounds you were surprised to hear?"

"There are sounds around us all the time which we are so used to hearing that we really don't hear them at all. *Too Much Noise* is about a man who was bothered by ordinary house sounds. Listen to how he solved his problem of too much noise." Read or tell the story.

PRESENTATION:

Introduce the puppets. If time permits allow a variety of children to manipulate each puppet.

Select the puppeteers. Ask them to experiment with ways of moving the puppet in character. "How does your animal move as it walks from the barn to the house? How does your puppet act in the house? How will you show that Peter is annoyed?"

As the puppeteers practice, the remainder of the group can experiment with their voices, the instruments and other materials to create the needed sound effects. Sounds could be assigned to individuals, pairs, or the whole group. Practice each sound before beginning the dramatization.

When everyone is in place, begin to narrate the story. If the children operating Peter or the Wise man want to speak the dialogue, encourage them to do so.

FOLLOW-UP:

1. Display other versions of the story.

> Chroman, Eleanor. *It Could Be Worse*. Children's Press, 1972.
> Dobbs, Rose. *No Room*. McKay, 1966.
> Hirsh, Marilyn. *Could Anything Be Worse?* Holiday House, 1974.
> Zemach, Margot. *It Could Always Be Worse*. Farrar, Straus, Giroux, 1976.

2. Introduce other stories in which sound is important, that is, in which the action of the story revolves around sound.

> Baylor, Byrd. *Plink plink plink*. Houghton Mifflin, 1971.
> Budney, Blossom. *After Dark*. Lothrop Lee & Shephard, 1975.
> Elkin, Benjamin. *The Loudest Noise in the World*. Viking, 1955.
> Wilson, Graham. *Bang Bang Family*. Scribner, 1974:

VARIATIONS:

1. Retell the story with different puppeteers. Provide only the narration and have the children provide the dialogue.

2. Dramatize another version of the story.

3. Brainstorm all the other sounds of a house that could bother Peter. Create a new version of the story using these sounds.

Paper Costumes

Children can work in pairs to create "people puppets" from heavy oak-tag for the human beings in the story—Farmer Peter, wise man, relatives. (One group of children decided to have a wise woman instead of a wise man.) One child lays down on the oak tag while the other traces a basic body shape. A hole will be cut for the child's face and hands. For primary children you will have to cut out the face and arm holes. Fabric scraps, construction and tissue paper, yarn, and other materials from your scrap box can be used to give the puppet individuality. The animals in the story can be done in this style or as large rod puppets.

When the puppets are completed, give children an opportunity to experiment with ways of moving the puppets in character. You might ask, "How does your animal move as it walks from the barn to the house? How does your puppet act in the house? How will you show that Peter is annoyed."

As the puppeteers practice, ask some of the children to decide how to make the sound effects needed—tea kettle whistling, leaves rustling, etc. Give them time to experiment with rhythm instruments and other materials, such as tissue paper, stones in a can. Sounds could be assigned to individuals, pairs, or the whole group. Practice each sound before beginning the dramatization.

Designate an area for the wise man's house and another for Peter's house. The area for the barnyard should be far enough away to give the puppeteers a chance to move freely as the animal characters. All the children making sound effects can sit on the floor in a fourth area.

Dramatizing the story with simple costumes and props.

SOUND AND ACTION

DRAMATIC ACTIVITY: Using sounds and actions to tell a story.

LITERATURE: An adaptation of Carolyn Bailey's story, *The Tree That Trimmed Itself*, the text of which follows.

TO THE LEADER : The addition of actions to a sound story is a natural development. Ask children to pantomime the actions indicated by the story, as well as to make the sounds. Do not show them how to do any specific action, but rather, let them discover ways for themselves. There may be a great variety of movements for any action in the story. If less secure children copy what others are doing, don't be concerned. In time, given encouragement and an uncritical atmosphere, the children will develop confidence enough to move in their own way.

Actions may be small and tentative the first time children do this type of activity. Continued opportunity to participate in dramatic activities will bring forth concentration and involvement.

PREPARATION: Practice telling or reading the story. Arrange book display.

INTRODUCTION: "What do you use to decorate your Christmas tree?" Allow children to respond.

PRESENTATION: "I know a story about a Christmas tree that trimmed itself—and the ornaments were very unusual. In order to tell this story I need your help."

"Whenever I raise my hands like this (demonstrate upward movement similar to that used by musical conductor), you make the sound or do the action described in the story. When I lower my hands (demonstrate), stop your activity. You'll need to listen and watch carefully. Do all the actions at your seat." You may feel confident enough to ask children to stand while doing the actions.

Tell the story giving hand signal to cue children's participation.

57

FOLLOW-UP:

1. Display books of holiday stories.

   Aleichem, Sholom. *Hanukah Money.* Morrow, 1978.

   Association for Childhood Education International. Literature Committee. *Told Under the Christmas Tree.* Macmillan, 1948.

   "The Tree That Trimmed Itself" appears on pages 41–44.

   Dasent, George W. *The Cat on the Doverfell: A Christmas Tale.* Putnam, 1978.

   Mendoza, George. *A Wart Snake in a Fig Tree.* Dial, 1968.

2. Display books about holiday customs.

   Barth, Edna. *Holly, Reindeer, and Colored Lights.* Seabury, 1971.

   Ets, Marie H. *Nine Days to Christmas.* Viking, 1959.

   Lindgren, Astrid. *Christmas in Noisy Village.* Viking, 1964.

3. Draw pictures of the tree that trimmed itself.

VARIATIONS:

1. Use hand puppets to portray the actions.

2. Tell the story doing the actions standing and moving in place.

3. Teach the children a traditional or nonsense verse, such as "Pease Porridge Hot." Ask them to say the rhyme in different ways:

   —fast
   —slow
   —with body movements (hand clapping, tapping shoulders)
   —with specific emotions (angry, sad, happy)
   —as a character, eg., "How would you say this rhyme if you were a witch brewing a spell? What would you do? How would you sound?"

4. Other stories suitable for sound and action participation include:

   Aardema, Verna. *Who's in Rabbit's House?* Dial, 1977.

   Brown, Margaret Wise. *The Golden Egg Book.* Simon and Schuster, 1947.

   Gerson, Mary-Joan. *Why the Sky is Far Away.* Harcourt, Brace, Jovanovich, 1974.

   McPhail, David. *The Bear's Toothache.* Little, Brown, 1972.

   Piper, Watty. *The Little Engine That Could.* Platt and Munk, 1961.

   Stern, Simon. *The Hobyahs.* Prentice Hall, 1977.

The Tree That Trimmed Itself

by Carolyn Bailey

(Suggested participation is marked with an *.)

The forest was very still and cold. Suddenly the silence was broken by chopping sounds as a woodsman cut down a large pine tree (*). He swung his ax swiftly and steadily (*). The tree swayed (*), cracked (*), and crashed to the ground (*). "This will make a beautiful Christmas tree," the woodsman thought as he tied the tree to his sled (*) and started for home (*).

A young pine tree nearby gave a sigh (*) as it watched the woodsman leave. "I wish, oh, I wish that I might be a Christmas tree with decorations like my brother who was cut down!"

Although it was Christmas Eve, very few trees had been cut for the children. The tall, strong trees were needed for building homes, kindling fires, making furniture. But, oh, the happiness of a Christmas tree sparkling in the light of a fireplace with children opening presents around it (*). No wonder that the young pine tree sighed (*) again in the wind.

"I wish that I might be trimmed for Christmas!" it whispered. At that moment white stars, shaped like shining crystals, came floating down among the outspread branches of the pine tree (*). More and still more stars fell (*), until every twig of every branch of the tree held its white star (*). They were more beautiful than any ornament that the toyman had for trimming a Christmas tree.

But still the young pine longed for all the honors his brother tree would have. "I wish that I might hear the Christmas Chimes!" it sighed (*) in the wind.

Then the night grew colder and colder. The frost came through the forest and stopped beside the pine tree (*), hanging sharp, hard icicles to the tips of the twigs (*).

Whenever the wind touched the tree the icicles tinkled (*) and rang (*) like a chime of tiny Christmas bells (*). They made soft, beautiful Christmas music (*).

But still the young pine tree was not satisfied. "I wish," it sighed (*), "that I might hold lights as my brother will on this Christmas Eve."

Suddenly the stars shone out in the darkness and dropped their beams of light down as far as the branches of the young pine tree (*). One star seemed to leave the sky and rest on the topmost twig of the Pine tree (*). There it flamed (*) and flashed (*) like a beacon to call everyone to see the wonders of Christmas Eve. The pine tree was lighted as brightly as if it carried a hundred candles, but still it had a wish.

"I am still not a Christmas Tree!" it sighed (*). "I wish that I might hold gifts among my branches." And it seemed as if this wish could never come true, for where could Christmas gifts be found in the wintry forest?

Christmas Eve changed to the very early dawning of Christmas Day. Still the Pine Tree wore its snow stars. Its icicle chimes rang (*) in the clear, cold air, and the light of the sky shone in its branches (*) like a Christmas light.

And from the shelter of a nest among its roots, a tiny mouse stuck out its head (*). The mouse was cold and hungry. He looked around hoping to find something to eat (*). Just above his head, the mouse saw (*) a bunch of berries hanging from a branch. He picked the berries (*) and began to eat them (*). What a nice Christmas gift, thought the mouse, as he finished the berries (*).

From the trunk of the Pine tree a squirrel peeked out (*). He, too, was hungry. The squirrel's claws made short, scrapping sounds (*) as he moved along the tree looking for something to eat (*). At the end of a branch he spied a fat, brown pine cone (*). Carefully the squirrel took the cone from the branch (*). He held the cone daintily in his paws (*), cut out the seeds (*), and munched them (*). It was his holiday breakfast and how good it tasted! No better Christmas gift could have come to the squirrel than that fat pine cone so full of seeds.

"Merry Christmas!" called the children (*), running to the woods (*) later on Christmas morning. "Merry Christmas, little pine tree. We have brought a bundle of grain for the snow bird (*). We saw his nest in your branches yesterday."

They reached up as far as they could (*) and hung the grain by a red ribbon to one of the branches of the pine tree (*). Then the children stood very quietly (*) and watched (*) as the snow bird came out of its nest to eat the grain (*).

"The pine tree has given the snow bird a warm winter home," the children said to each other (*). Then they left the forest (*).

And the little pine tree stood straight and happy in the woods on Christmas morning (*), for all of its wishes had come true. It had trimmed itself with stars (*), heard the chimes (*) and had offered its gifts to its friends.

60

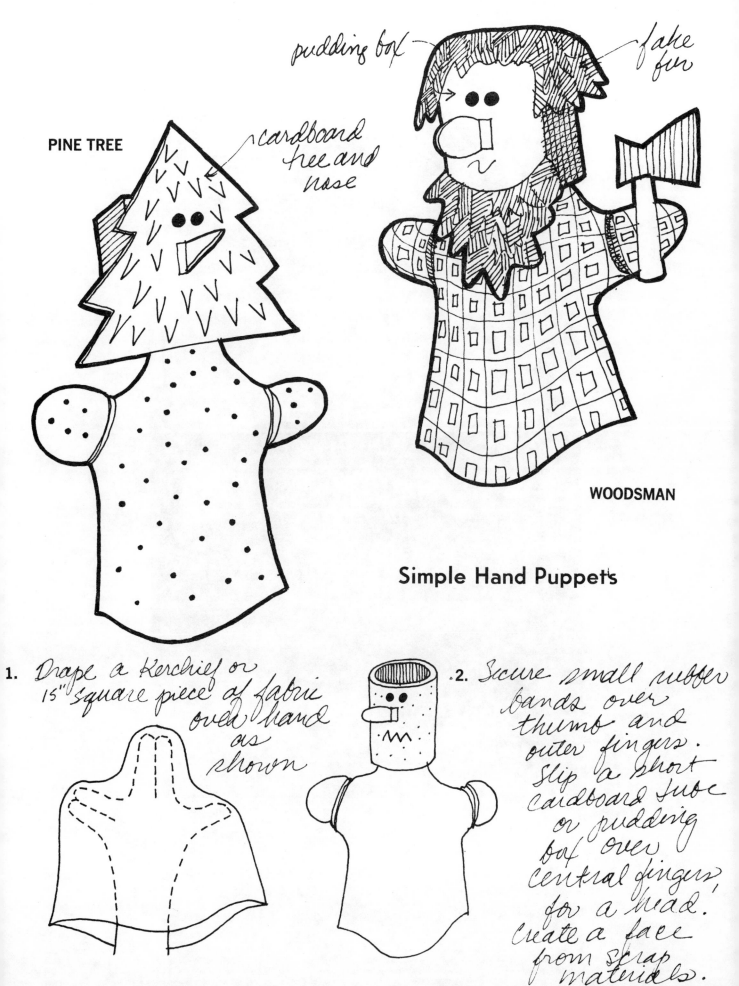

pudding box

fake fur

PINE TREE

cardboard tree and nose

WOODSMAN

Simple Hand Puppets

1. Drape a kerchief or 15" square piece of fabric over hand as shown

2. Secure small rubber bands over thumb and outer fingers. Slip a short cardboard tube or pudding box over central fingers for a head. Create a face from scrap materials.

SEQUENCE GAME

DRAMATIC ACTIVITY: Utilizing pantomime and dialogue to convey a story line.

LITERATURE: Display biographies of characters mentioned in the game: *Benjamin Franklin, John Paul Jones, Buffalo Bill, Annie Oakley, Marie Mitchell, Harriet Tubman, Frederick Douglass, George Washington Carver, Thomas Edison, Sitting Bull, Walter Reed, Houdini, Maria Tallchief, Chris Evert, Leonard Bernstein, Gordon Parks.*

TO THE LEADER: In sequence games children interpret book related activities through dialogue and pantomime. Each child receives one or two cards with dialogue and/or pantomime activities printed on them. During the game children perform the activities in their proper sequence. The cards tell them what to do; the children do the activity in their own way.

The game is structured and involves everyone—those not doing an activity are listening and watching intently for their cue. This game is a good activity for use with upper elementary children who have not had much exposure to creative dramatics.

PREPARATION: Make the game cards. (Sample text, at end). Print the activities in black and the cues in red. The "cue" message was the "you" message on the card given to the preceding person in the sequence.

CUE: Jump and say, "How did he do that?" Sit. (Typed in red)
YOU: Stand and say, "That's why they call him the great Houdini." Sit. (Typed in black)

PHYSICAL SETTING: Children sit in large circle on the floor.

INTRODUCTION: "Can anyone explain what is meant by biography?" Encourage children to discuss biographies they have read.

PRESENTATION: "Today we're going to play a game based on biography."

Ask the children to sit in a circle on the floor. Pass out the sequence cards in a random manner. Some children may get more than one card.

Explain that the cue section written in red tells what the person before has done or said. You may say, "When you see that activity done, get set to do your activity next." Tell children to do what is written in the *you* section and to say only what is written in quotation marks. Encourage the children to do the activity and say the words "as if" they are the famous person.

Have everybody read their cards silently. Ask children to raise their hands if they do not know a word or do not understand a direction. Quietly give the needed assistance. The child who has the card that says, "You begin the game," goes into the center of the circle and does the required activity.

You will follow the game's progress on the master sheet. If someone misses a cue, describe what has just been done. If no one responds, state the next action and ask if anyone has that card. At the end of the game, collect all cards and briefly discuss the biography book display.

FOLLOW-UP:
1. Display biographies based on the characters in the game.

   Aulaire, Ingri D. *Buffalo Bill*. Doubleday, 1955.
   Cone, Molly. *Leonard Bernstein*. Crowell, 1970.
   Edwards, Anne. *Great Houdini*. Putnam, 1977.
   Gridley, Marion. *Maria Tallchief*. Dillon Press, 1973.
   Smith, J. *Chris Evert*. Children's Press, 1975.
   Towne, Peter. *George Washington Carver*. Crowell, 1975.

2. Display biographies of other famous people in a particular area such as sports.

   Robinson, Nancy. *Janet Guthrie: Race Car Driver*. Children's Press, 1979.
   Smith, M. *Dorothy Hamill*. Children's Press, 1977.

Talbert, Peter. *Tracy Austin Tennis Wonder*. Putnam, 1979.

VARIATIONS:

1. Interpret the game through plastic bottle puppets.
2. Use a whole book or poem as the basis of a sequence game.

   BOOK: Seuling, Barbara. *The Teeny Tiny Woman*. Viking Press, 1976.
   POEM: Bodecker, N. M. "Let's Marry, Said the Cherry." In N. M. Bodecker, *Let's Marry, Said the Cherry*. Atheneum, 1974.

3. Introduce fables, tall tales, or folklore by way of a sequence game.
4. Write a sequence game based on one chapter or incident from a book.

SEQUENCE GAME—BIOGRAPHY—SAMPLE CARDS SUGGESTIONS

1. You begin the game. Stand and say, "May I have your attention please? The Parade of Famous Americans is about to begin." Bow and sit down.

2. Stand and say, "In the year 1706 an American of many talents was born in Boston." Sit.

3. Stand and say, *"Ben Franklin* made a success of nearly everything he tried. And he tried nearly everything." Sit.

4. Stand and say, "He published a magazine called *POOR RICHARD'S ALMANAC* containing wise sayings." Sit.

5. Stand, walk around the circle saying, "Early to bed and early to rise makes a man healthy, wealthy, and wise." Return to your seat.

6. Stand, scratch head and say, "Why didn't I think of that." Sit.

7. Stand, clear throat, and say, "Being an author, printer, inventor, scientist, ambassador, and statesman did keep me rather busy." Bow and sit down.

8. Stand and say in an impressed voice, "WOW!" Sit down.

9. Stand and say proudly, "I'm *Captain John Paul Jones*. During the Revolutionary War, I sailed under the motto CONQUER OR DIE." Sit down.

10. Stand and say, "It's no wonder he's known as the Father of the United States Navy." Sit down.

11. Stand, load a rifle, shoot and then say, "Shooting was always easy for me. That's why *Buffalo Bill* made me a star in his Wild West Show." Smile and sit down.

12. Stand, shake hands with person who just sat down and say, *"Annie Oakley,* you sure deserved the title QUEEN OF THE RIFLE." Return to your seat.

13. Stand, look through a telescope as if searching for something. Turn head away, look again, then shout, "I've never seen that comet before." Sit down.

14. Stand and say, *"Marie Mitchell* was only 28 when she discovered that new comet in 1847." Sit down.

15
16 } Stand, walk around circle as if you're afraid of being followed.
17

Say, "Going North, going North, going North on the

Underground Railroad." Sit (Three of you will do this.)

18. Stand and say, "I'm *Harriet Tubman* and before 1865 I helped many slaves travel to freedom on the Underground Railroad." Sit down.

19. Stand and say, "Why am I a slave? Why are some people slaves and others masters? Why, Why?" Sit down.

20. Stand and say, *"Frederick Douglass* kept asking those questions. He was a friend of *Abraham Lincoln's* and a leader of the Black people during the Civil War." Sit down.

21. Stand, open door to barn, look around and say, "Peanuts here, peanuts there, peanuts, peanuts everywhere. What am I going to do with all these peanuts?" Return to seat.

22. Stand and say, "I think I can help. My name is *George Washington Carver* and I've got recipes for peanut milk, peanut flour, peanut cardboard, peanut face cream, and 300 other things." Bow and sit down.

23. Stand and say, "I'm an inventor too, but I can't make anything from peanuts." Shake head sadly and sit down.

24. Stand, walk over to person who just sat down, pat person on back and say, "Don't worry *Thomas Edison,* your phonograph, electric light, and motion picture inventions are very popular." Return to your seat.

25. Stand and say, "The year is 1876 and I, *Sitting Bull,* Chief of the Sioux, must lead my people to safety in Canada. After the battle against Custer at the Little Big Horn, the white men will never leave the Indian in Peace." Sit down.

26. Stand, put hand to forehead, and say, "Oh, I've got an awful headache and I'm so hot. I must be sick." Lie down. (Return to your seat after someone says, "I'll do an experiment to find out.")

27. Stand, rush to person lying down, feel person's forehead and say, "It's yellow fever. What causes yellow fever? I wonder if all those mosquitoes have anything to do with it. I'll do an experiment to find out." Return to your seat.

28. Stand and say, *"Walter Reed* did his experiment and proved that yellow fever is caused by mosquitoes." Sit down.

29. Stand, pretend to be in a locked closet with your hands in handcuffs behind your back and your legs chained together. Pretend to escape, then smile, bow and return to your seat.

30. Jump up and say, "How did he do that?" Sit down.

31. Stand and say, "It's no wonder they call him *THE GREAT HOUDINI."* Sit.

32. Stand and say, "My name is *Maria Tallchief* and I am an American Indian. I always loved to dance but it was still hard work to become a prima ballerina." Sit down.

33. Stand and say, "All the members of Maria's tribe were so proud of her, they made her an Indian Princess." Sit down.

34. Stand, pretend to be swinging a tennis racket and say, "The time is now. *Chris Evert's* the name and tennis is my game." Sit.

35. Stand, pretend you are conducting an orchestra, and say, "I love music-writing it, playing it, and conducting it." Bow and sit down.

36. Stand and applaud. Then sit down.

37. Stand, applaud, and then say, "That was *Leonard Bernstein* conducting. Maybe you've seen him on TV." Sit down.

38. Stand, walk around taking photos. Say, "Taking pictures is only one part of my life. I also write music, books, and poems. Maybe you saw the movie about my life called, *THE LEARNING TREE.*" Sit down.

39. Stand and say, *"Gordon Parks* was the first Black man to produce and direct a movie for a big company. He opened the way for other Blacks to do the same thing." Sit down.

40. Stand and say, "These are only a few of the people who make America great. Your friendly librarian will be happy to tell you about others." Sit.

41. Stand and announce, "Books about all these famous people can be found in the biography section of the _____ *Great School* Library." Sit.

42. Stand and say, "Hurry and check one out while the supply lasts." Sit.

Making
The Puppets

paper cylinder hat

fake fur or yarn hair

rubber cement or scotch tape features to bottle

attach old clothing to wire hanger shoulders

cardboard hands

stuff clothing with crumpled newspaper

ABE LINCOLN

cardboard or real shoes

Plastic-Bottle Puppets

1. Wash out thoroughly a plastic bottle (milk, liquid soap, clorox, etc).
2. Create features on opposite surface from handle.
3. Tape coat hanger wire into neck of bottle (or insert into neck), for shoulders.

hold puppet by handle

Puppet idea by Frank Wickham, 6th grade teacher
Laura Dodge Elementary School, Omaha, NE

INTERVIEW

DRAMATIC ACTIVITY: Developing characterization through dialogue.

TO THE LEADER: Children will develop a clearer understanding of a character by responding to questions "as if" they were that character. The interview situation provides a framework within which the child can respond as a specific character. It is important to give children this framework in which to interpret their character. Providing guidance will help children to be at ease and free to use their imagination. To ask children to become characters and then to allow them to talk about anything they choose will produce very little creative action. Too much freedom can be as stifling as too little.

INTRODUCTION: "If I said I was going to interview you, what would you expect me to do? Yes, ask questions. A reporter interviewing a famous person or a new student at school are good examples."

Discuss reason for interviewing someone and the types of questions you might ask. Set up an interview situation using, if possible, a suggestion from the group. Let one child assume the role of the person to be interviewed. Everyone else will be an interviewer. A newspaper or TV reporter interviewing a personality of the children's choice provides a good framework for the interview. Complete the interview.

PRESENTATION: Divide the group into partners, A and B. A becomes a favorite book character. B interviews the character finding out as much as possible about the character. Remind A to answer in the way the character would. Encourage interviewers to ask characters how they felt about story incidents or why they behaved as they did.

Switch. B now becomes character interviewed by A.

Let children share with the group some of the things they learned about each character.

FOLLOW-UP:

1. Ask each child to find the book in which their character appears. Display these for others to examine.

2. Tape some of the interviews and let the children listen to themselves. If the partners agree, share the interview with the group.

VARIATIONS:

1. Give each child a sock puppet, whose only feature is two dots for eyes. Partners use these anonymous sock puppets to interview each others' puppet. After the interview, each child finishes the puppet as the determined character.

2. A is a story character. B must discover who A is through questions. This game can also be played with the whole group asking questions.

3. Pin character names on backs of children. Children ask each other questions to discover their identity. All questions must have yes or no answers, such as: Am I a girl?; Am I a fairy tale character?

Names which can be used include:
For Younger Children

Mother Goose

Little Miss Muffet

Old Mother Hubbard

Old King Cole

Spider

Humpty Dumpty

Jack Be Nimble

Peter Peter Pumpkin Eater

Wolf

Grandmother

Little Red Riding Hood

Jack in the Beanstalk

Giant

Cinderella

Gingerbread Boy

Goldilocks

Baby Bear

Mama Bear

Papa Bear

Georgie the Ghost

Troll

Small Billy Goat Gruff

Middle Billy Goat Gruff

Big Billy Goat Gruff

Cat in the Hat

Curious George

For Older Children

Annabel in *Freaky Friday*

Aslan in *The Lion, the Witch and the Wardrobe*

Bilbo in *The Hobbit*

Caddie in *Caddie Woodlawn*

Charlotte in *Charlotte's Web*

Chester in *Cricket in Times Square*

Fudge in *Tales of a Fourth Grade Nothing*

Harriet in *Harriet the Spy*

Henry in *Henry Huggins*

Homer in *Homer Price*

James in *James and the Giant Peach*

Laura in *Little House* Series

Long John Silver in *Treasure Island*

Mrs. Basil E. Frankweiler in *From the Mixed-Up Files of Mrs. Basil E. Frankweiler*

Mary Poppins in *Mary Poppins* series

Meg in *Wrinkle in Time*

Milo in *The Phantom Tollbooth*

Paddington in *A Bear Called Paddington*

Pippi in *Pippi Longstocking*

Pod in *The Borrowers* series

Characters from mythology could also be used as the basis for this activity.

As students discover who they are, they pin the character name on their front and begin moving as the character.

When everyone knows who they are let children group themselves according to books or stories. If you feel comfortable with the idea, ask groups to share one thing that happened in their book. To help children understand, you might say, "In your group pick one event that happened in the story that you'd like to share."

4. Older children enjoy this activity. Divide children into groups of five. Each group goes to a table in order to decide on a story. You may place books on each table as suggestions but allow children to make their own story choice. Within the group each child selects a character from the chosen story.

Ask one group to sit or stand as its characters. The rest of the children will try to discover what story the group represents. Only questions which can be answered with a "yes" or "no" may be asked. Allow twenty questions. Encourage children to answer questions "as if" they were the character. If there is a long silence between questions, you ask a question such as, "Is the story a folktale?"

Before beginning, discuss the types of questions which will provide helpful information, such as questions about setting, characters, plot, and literature genre. Let children experiment with asking questions in these areas which require a yes or a no answer.

As a warm-up you might be a character and let children question you to discover your identity. Answer the questions using a voice, gestures, mannerisms, and body movements suitable for your character.

Popular titles include:

Baum, Frank. *The Wizard of Oz*. Macmillan, 1962.

Dahl, Roald. *Charlie and the Chocolate Factory*. Alfred A. Knopf, 1964.

Grimm, Jacob and Wilhelm. *Snow-White and the Seven Dwarfs*. Translated By Randall Jarrell. Farrar, Straus and Giroux, 1972.

Milne, A. A. *Winnie-the-Pooh*. Dutton, 1926.

Tolkien, J. R. R. *The Hobbit*. Houghton Mifflin, 1938.

Wadsworth, Wallace. *Paul Bunyan and His Great Blue Ox*. Doubleday, 1964.

White, E. B. *Charlotte's Web*. Harper and Row, 1952.

buttons, paper or
painted
eyes

Tuck in toe of sock
to form a mouth.
Sew or staple corners
to help define mouth.

ANONYMOUS CHARACTERS

Create anonymous
puppets from socks.
After interviews, have
children complete puppet
characters.

COMPLETED CHARACTERS

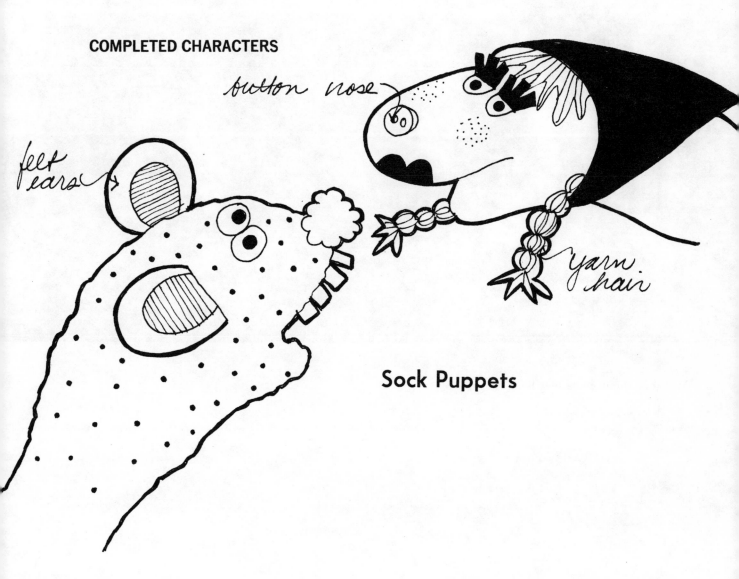

button nose

felt ears

yarn hair

Sock Puppets

77

Monkeys Mumble in a Jelly Bean Jungle

FROZEN PICTURES

DRAMATIC ACTIVITY: Using dramatic action to bring illustrations to life.

LITERATURE: Scheer, Julian. *Rain Makes Applesauce.* Holiday House, 1964.

TO THE LEADER: *Rain Makes Applesauce* is a beautifully illustrated picture book of delightful absurdities. The images presented are vivid and very appealing to children. Children simultaneously create their interpretation of each image. Making a still picture aids concentration and eliminates concern over how to begin and end. Bringing the picture to life for a few seconds is sufficient for most children who have had little experience with creative dramatics and movement.

This technique can also be used for a complete playing of a single action of a character. From working alone, children can progress to working in pairs. The picture can be brought to life when music is heard and refrozen when the music ends.

PHYSICAL SETTING: Clear, open space.

PREPARATION: Write the following sentences from *Rain Makes Applesauce* on cards.

> Dolls Go Dancing On the Moon
>
> My House Goes Walking Everyday
>
> The Wind Blows Backwards All Night Long
>
> Monkeys Mumble in a Jelly Bean Jungle
>
> Candy Tastes Like Soap, Soap, Soap
>
> Tigers Sleep on an Elephant Snoot
>
> Monkeys Eat the Chimney Smoke

Clouds Hide in a Hole in the Sky

My Teddy Bear Sings Out Loud at Night

Rain Makes Applesauce

INTRODUCTION:

"Illustrators use paint, brushes, ink, and many other materials to create pictures for books. But there's another way of making pictures—using your bodies. Stand up and try making some still pictures using your body. I'll tell you the name of a picture. Then I'll close my eyes and count to ten as you make the picture. When I open my eyes, freeze and don't move unless I push a magic button and bring your picture to life. Show me someone:

throwing a ball

shoveling snow

flying a kite."

"Now find a space in the room where you do not touch anyone else. I'm going to give you the title of an illustration needed for the book *Rain Makes Applesauce*. Try to make the most interesting picture using your body as you can. The first one is, 'Dolls Go Dancing on the Moon.' "
Close your eyes and count to ten. Walk around and look at the pictures making positive comments. Stop at a few and turn them on. After the picture has come to life for a few seconds switch it off. If some children are not ready to bring their pictures to life just turn them off and move on. Never force a child to participate; when ready, each child will become involved.

For active titles, such as the wind blowing backwards, ask children to bring the picture to life in slow motion. This will strengthen their concentration in addition to helping you keep control. For some titles you may want to bring all the pictures to life simultaneously.

After creating pictures for titles you supply, give the children an opportunity to create an original picture and give it a title. Have half the class present their pictures while the other half watches, then switch.

FOLLOW-UP:

1. Show the book *Rain Makes Applesauce*. Encourage children to compare the illustration in the book to the one they imagined and created with their body.

2. Display other books of silly talk and absurdities:

Anno, Mitsumasa. *Topsy-Turvies*. Weatherhill, 1970.

Anno, Mitsumasa. *Upside-Downers*. Weatherhill, 1971.

Charlip, Remy. *Arm in Arm*. Parents' Magazine Press, 1969.

Charlip, Remy and Jerry Joyner. *Thirteen*. Parents' Magazine Press, 1975.

Kraus, Ruth. *A Hole is to Dig*. Harper, 1952.

VARIATIONS:

1. Individuals work alone to create a picture from a book. Show an illustration. Ask children, "What is happening? What do you think will happen next?" Then ask children to create a frozen picture of the illustration. Bring the pictures to life with a drum beat or other signal. Have children freeze when they have completed the character's action.

Books which can be used include:

Bond, Michael. *A Bear Called Paddington*. Houghton Mifflin, 1958.

De Paola, Tomi. *Strega Nona*. Prentice-Hall, 1975.

McCloskey, Robert. *Burt Dow Deep-Water Man*. Viking Press, 1963.

Seuss, Dr. *The 500 Hats of Bartholomew Cubbins*. Vanguard, 1938.

2. In groups of two or three, ask children to create frozen pictures based on an illustration which they then bring to life. When the children have completed the action they freeze.

Titles which have appropriate illustrations:

Baker, Betty. *Partners*. Greenwillow, 1978.

Coville, Bruce. *The Foolish Giant*. Lippincott, 1978.

Galdone, Paul. *Androcles and the Lion*. McGraw Hill, 1970.

Ginsburg, Mirra. *Mushroom in the Rain*. Macmillan, 1974.

Steig, William. *Sylvester and the Magic Pebble*. 1969.

3. Create titles for pictures depicting fantasy characters in action. Ask children to create a frozen picture for each title. Possible titles include:

—Chester, the cricket, Gives a Concert
—The Last of the Great Whangdoodles
—Mary Poppins Floats Over Rooftops
—A Ride in Chitty-Chitty Bang-Bang.

Dolls Go Dancing On the Moon

Candy Tastes Like Soap, Soap, Soap

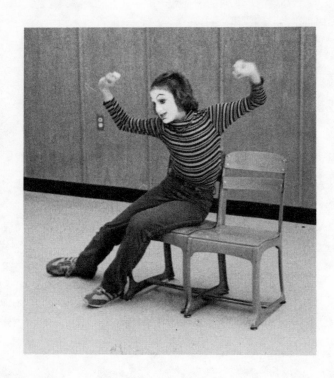

ACTIVITY PANTOMIME

DRAMATIC ACTIVITY: Pantomiming a character in action.

LITERATURE: Gag, Wanda. *Gone is Gone*. Coward-McCann, 1935.

TO THE LEADER : *Gone is Gone* is a folktale in which a husband complains about how difficult his work is and decides to change jobs with his wife. The switch doesn't prove to be to his liking.

To do activity pantomime, children select an action and do it "as if" they have become the character. Stories in which one character has a series of adventures are well suited for activity pantomime. This is a good beginning step towards characterization. It is not necessary for children to try activities in sequence. Before beginning, establish a control signal. This can be a simple clap of the hands followed by the word "freeze."
If pantomiming, a variety of character actions results in the children showing an interest and desire to continue, you may narrate as the children join the activities together.

PHYSICAL SETTING: Clear, open space.

PREPARATION: Practice telling or reading the story. Collect and arrange books for display.

INTRODUCTION: "Being a farmer is very hard work because there are always chores to do. What are the jobs a farmer must do?" List the chores as the children name them. Ask children to pantomime some of the chores.
"I know a farmer who thought it would be much easier to care for his house and baby instead of working in the fields. So he switched jobs with his wife and this is what happened."

PRESENTATION: Tell or read *Gone is Gone*.

"What chores did Fritzl do in the fields?" (Plow, sow, hoe, etc.) After each chore is named, ask the children to do that job as if they are Fritzl.

"What chores did Liesi have to do in the house?" (Clean, cook, churn butter, etc.) Give children time to do the chore as if they are Liesi.

"Now try doing Liesi's same chores as if you are Fritzl. Will you do the chore in the same way? How will your actions differ?" Name the chore and give children time to pantomime it. Signal children to freeze before naming the next chore.

"Do you think Fritzl continued complaining about his work in the fields?"

FOLLOW-UP: 1. Display other versions of the same story:

> Haviland, Virginia. *The Fairy Tale Treasury*. Coward-McCann and Geoghegan, 1972. Pp. 48–55.
>
> McKee, David. *The Man Who Was Going to Mind the House*. Abelard-Schuman, 1973.
>
> Wiesner, William. *Turnabout*. Seabury, 1972.

VARIATIONS: 1. Create body puppets to perform story.

2. Divide the children into two groups. Group A will be Liesi doing her household chores. Group B will be Fritzl doing the same chore. Group A will begin doing the chore you name. At a signal, such as a drum beat, or clapped hands, Group A will freeze and Group B will do the chore as if they are Fritzl. Alternate the action naming different chores.

If there is time, let Group A be Fritzl and Group B be Liesi.

3. Other books which can be used for activity pantomime experiences include:

> Burningham, John. *Time To Get Out of the Bath, Shirley*. T. Y. Crowell, 1978.
>
> Keats, Ezra Jack. *The Snowy Day*. Viking, 1963.
>
> Lasker, Joe. *Mothers Can Do Anything*. Whitman, 1972.
>
> Pearson, Susan. *Monday I Was an Alligator*. Lippincott, 1979.
>
> Ryan, Cheli. *Hildilid's Night*. Macmillan, 1971.
>
> Sperry, Armstrong. *Call It Courage*. Macmillan, 1940.

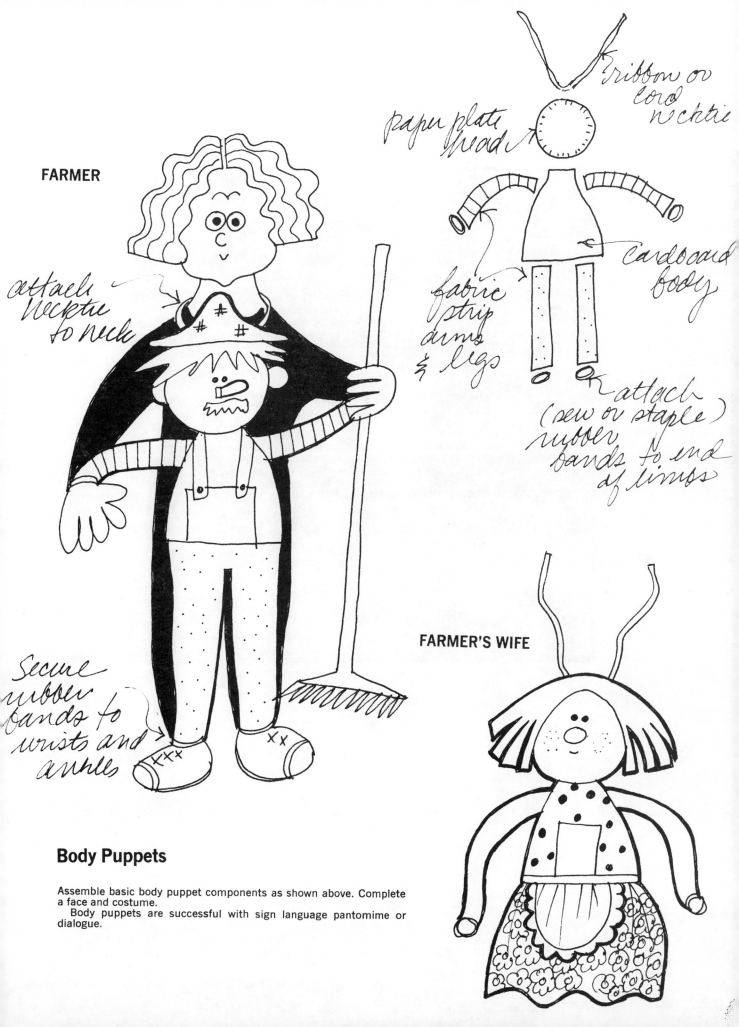

FARMER

attach necktie to neck

Secure rubber bands to wrists and ankles

paper plate head

ribbon or cord necktie

fabric strip arms & legs

cardboard body

attach (sew or staple) rubber bands to end of limbs

FARMER'S WIFE

Body Puppets

Assemble basic body puppet components as shown above. Complete a face and costume.

Body puppets are successful with sign language pantomime or dialogue.

NARRATIVE PANTOMIME

DRAMATIC ACTIVITY: Becoming a character involved in the action of the story.

LITERATURE: Mosel, Arlene. *The Funny Little Woman*. Dutton, 1972.

TO THE LEADER: The Caldecott award book *The Funny Little Woman* is a humorous folktale with a strong plot and vivid characters. The scene of the funny little woman escaping from the Oni is suitable for narrative pantomime because it is filled with interesting action. All the children may assume the character of the Oni and interpret the action in their own ways, as the story is read.

Texts which present strong visual images as well as continuous and uncomplicated action are especially suitable for narrative pantomime. Before using a selection, eliminate descriptive sections unnecessary to the forward movement of the action. Also, edit out any reference to the past or future since they would detract from the immediate impact of the story. In some cases, you can add to the dramatic appeal of the material by supplying details which will stimulate the children's thinking.

Children should be free to create the characters and action in their own way. They should feel relatively secure, since all are participating at the same time. You have given them interesting action and characters, as well as structure. The story outlines what to do; the child's challenge is to create the action in his or her own way.

PREPARATION: Assemble record player and record *Adventures in Music*, Grade 2, RCA Victor. For the pantomime use "Bydlo" from "Pictures at an Exhibition" by Modeste Moussorgsky, side 1, band 4.

Arrange book display.

**PHYSICAL
SETTING:** Clear, open space.

INTRODUCTION: "Do you know how to giggle? Let me hear you."

"I know a funny little woman who giggles so much that she sometimes gets herself into trouble. I'll tell her story if you'll help by supplying the funny little woman's giggle. When I raise my hands, you giggle. When I lower my hands, stop. Let's practice."

Tell the story using the book.

PRESENTATION: Allow children an opportunity to give their reactions to the Oni. Discuss the story: Why didn't the Oni want the funny little woman to run away? How did they try to stop her? What made the Oni laugh?

"Let's play that part of the story." Indicate area for the river. "You will be the Oni and we will imagine the funny little woman. Remember what happened in the story when the funny little woman tried to escape. If you were an Oni how would your feet feel as you walked in the mud? Show me how you would walk as an Oni."

"Good. Freeze. How would you swallow the river?" After the children have completed the action ask them to sink into the mud.

"When the music starts, slowly grow into an Oni. I will tell the last part of the story as you act it out. What will you do as Oni when the funny little woman is safely back in her home?" Let each child decide on an ending—they may want to return to their own home or become so angry that they stomp themselves into the mud. Ask the children to bring the scene to an end when the music finishes.

"In your own space make yourself as small as possible. When you hear the music, begin to grow into an Oni."

Children play the scene as you narrate the action. Watch the children as you narrate and adjust your storytelling to their pace.

FOLLOW-UP: 1. Display Japanese folklore.

Hodges, Margaret. *The Wave.* Houghton Mifflin, 1964.

Say, Allen. *Once Under a Cherry Blossom Tree.* Harper, 1974.

90

Stamm, Claus, reteller. *The Dumplings and the Demons*. Viking, 1964.

A tale similar to the *Funny Little Woman* concerning an old man, demons, and Jizo in the underground.

2. Introduce other outstanding Caldecott books.

DeRegniers, Beatrice Schenk. *May I Bring a Friend?* Illus. by Beni Montresori. Atheneum, 1964.

Langstaff, John. *Frog Went A-Courtin'*. Illus. by Feodor Rojankovsky. Harcourt, Brace and World, 1955.

Ness, Evaline. *Sam, Bangs and Moonshine*. Holt, Rinehart and Winston, 1966.

Zemach, Harve. *Duffy and the Devil*. Illus. by Margot Zemach. Farrar, Strauss, Giroux, 1973.

3. Other titles suitable for narrative pantomime include:

Boynton, Sandra. *Hester in the Wild*. Harper, 1979.
Children can pantomime each of Hester's adventures as you narrate them.

DiNoto, Andrea. *The Star Thief*. MacMillan, 1967.
Narrate the sections involving the thief stealing and hiding the stars, villagers up to their noses in stars and the thief trying to make the stars stick to the sky.

Edmonds, Walter D. *The Story of Richard Storm*. Little, Brown, 1974.
A step by step account of the growth of a storm provides the opportunity for a unique pantomime experience.

Haley, Gail E. *A Story, a Story*. Atheneum, 1970.
All children can play simultaneously as you narrate Anansi climbing to the sky, binding leopard, creeping towards hornet's nest; carving wooden doll and covering it with sticky latex gum, watching fairy dance around doll, and pulling captive to the sky.

Other stories about Anansi can be found in *Anansi the Spider* by Gerald McDermott (Holt Rinehart & Winston, 1972) and *The Hat-Shaking Dance and Other Ashanti Tales From Ghana* by Harold Courlander (Harcourt Brace Jovanovich, 1957).

Hoban, Russell. *Dinner at Alberta's*. Crowell, 1975.
Children will enjoy playing the scene of Albert eating with terrible table manners. Then they can play the section describing his new manners.

Hutchins, Pat. *Happy Birthday, Sam*. Greenwillow, 1978.
As you tell the story, children can pantomime Sam's unsuccessful attempts to reach ordinary places, such as a light switch and sink. A special

birthday present enables Sam to solve his reaching problems.

Krasilovsky, Phyllis. *The Man Who Didn't Wash His Dishes.*
The problems a man faces when he doesn't wash the dishes are described in this humorous story. Children can portray the man as he struggles to get rid of the dirty dishes.

Walsh, Jill Paton. *Toolmaker.* Seabury, 1973.
Older children can become involved in the sections describing how the tools are crafted.

VARIATIONS:

1. Create body costumes to dramatize the story.

2. Replay the scene with you or a child taking the part of the funny little woman.

3. Compare a subject as described in several poems. For example, cats as described in "Cat," "The Looking Glass Kitty," and "A Kitten Cornered." ·Each cat has unique qualities which will become clarified through pantomime.

Ask children to close their eyes and imagine each cat as you read the poems. Then reread each poem slowly and with expression as the children pantomime the cat's movements. Read and pantomime one poem before going on to another poem. "The Looking Glass Kitty" can be done in pairs.

Merriam, Eve. "Kitten Cornered." In Eve Merriam, *Outloud.* Atheneum, 1973. P. 18.

Miller, Mary Britton. "Cat." In John Brewton (Ed.), *Under the Tent of the Sky.* Macmillan, 1937. P. 76.

Widdemer, Margaret. "The Looking Glass Kitty." In John Brewton (Ed.), *Under the Tent of the Sky.* Macmillan, 1937. P. 75.

Growing Into An Oni

1. lay child down on large sheet of mural paper.
2. Draw a costume shape, larger than child's body.
3. cut out two identical shapes
4. staple upper sections of shapes together and flip costume over child (leave sides free)

METHOD 1

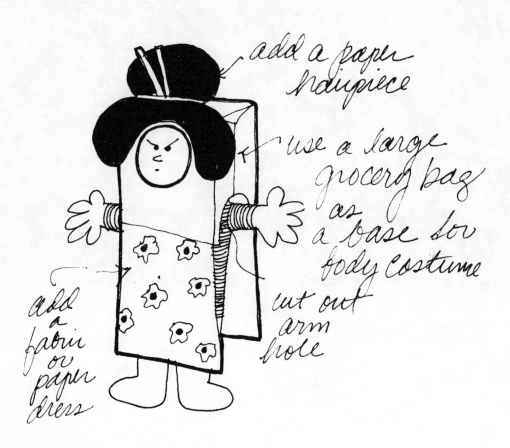

add a paper hairpiece

use a large grocery bag as a base for body costume

cut out arm hole

add a fabric or paper dress

METHOD 2

ONI

paper fringed hair

rubber cement paper claws to fingers

paint or use wallpaper for costume

THE FUNNY WOMAN

Paper Costumes

GROUP CREATIONS

DRAMATIC ACTIVITY: Creating a machine character with life and pulse.

LITERATURE: Burton, Virginia. *Mike Mulligan and his Steam Shovel*. Houghton, 1939.

TO THE LEADER: Creating machine creatures from a story offers children the opportunity to work creatively and cooperatively with others, in addition to providing opportunities for developing a variety of body movements and rhythms. For this activity, select a story in which a machine plays an integral part in the plot and conflict, such as Mary Ann in *Mike Mulligan and His Steam Shovel*.

Before asking children to work together to create a machine, discuss how the machine works. Let children contribute their ideas regarding parts of the machine. While still sitting, encourage children to make a variety of mechanical movements using only their hands.
After the machine character has been developed children may act out sections of the story.

PHYSICAL SETTING: Clear, open space.

INTRODUCTION: Read the book *Mike Mulligan and His Steam Shovel* to the group.

"How is Mary Ann different from most characters in books?" Examine the diagram in the book which labels the parts of a machine shovel.

"If we were going to build a steam shovel like Mary Ann what parts would we need?" As each part is named, ask children to move their arms corresponding to the part.

"In this story Mary Ann must be able to move dirt very quickly. Which of her parts is most important for digging?"

"Stand up. In your own space, become Mary Ann's digging arm. When I give the signal, start digging the basement. Begin slowly, as Mary Ann did, and gradually increase your speed until the basement is finished. Then relax and look over your work."

PRESENTATION: Give a signal, such as a clap of your hands, and narrate Mary Ann's digging as the children do the digging.

In small group of two or three, ask the children to use their bodies to create Mary Ann. Without climbing onto one another, have them work together to create Mary Ann.

"Be sure Mary Ann can move her digging arm. When you're ready, we'll play the part of the story in which Mary Ann digs the basement of the town hall."

FOLLOW-UP: Give children a few minutes to make their group version of Mary Ann. When they are ready narrate the building section, omitting extraneous description and dialogue.

1. Display other books with machine characters:

Gramatky, Hardie. *Little Toot*. Putnam, 1939.

Gramatky, Hardie. *Loopy*. Putnam, 1939.

Lenski, Lois. *The Little Auto*. Walck, 1934.

VARIATIONS: 1. Create a machine puppet.

2. Other stories which have machine characters that could be made as group creations include:

Brown, Margaret Wise. *The Steamroller*. Walker, 1974.

Burton, Virginia Lee. *Katy and the Big Snow*. Houghton Mifflin, 1943.

Gramatky, Hardie. *Hercules*. Putnam, 1940.

McCloskey, Robert. *Homer Price*. Viking, 1943.

3. Working in pairs, ask the children to create fantasy characters, such as the monsters in *One Monster After Another* by Mercer Mayer, Golden Press, 1974.

98

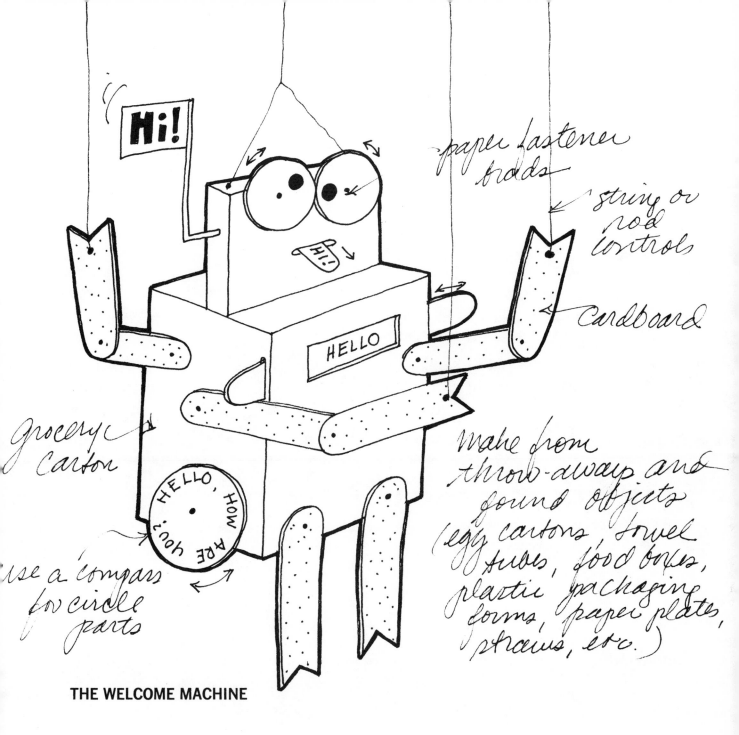

THE WELCOME MACHINE

Create an animated machine that has a special function and that is unlike other machines, such as:

A machine that walks on ceilings and walls.
A machine that *loves* to do homework.
A machine that serves as an ambassador to other countries or planets.

Develop a voice and movements appropriate to the machine's function.

HEAD WORN MACHINE

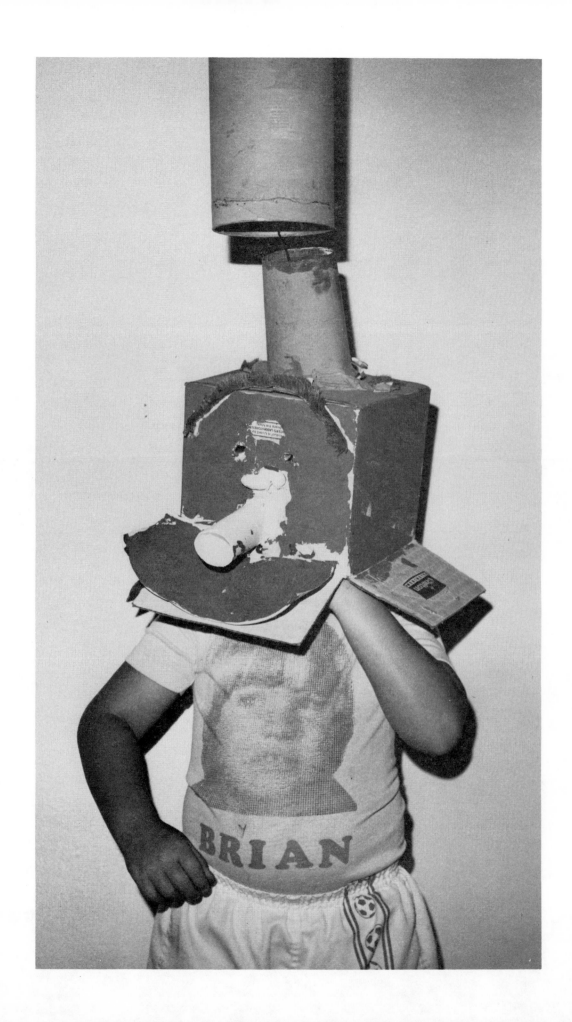

CREATE THE WHERE

DRAMATIC ACTIVITY: Using imagination to create the story environment.

LITERATURE: Norton, Mary. *The Borrowers*. Harcourt, Brace, Jovanovich, Inc. 1953.

TO THE LEADER: *The Borrowers* is a fantasy about little creatures who live in old houses—under clocks, over mantles, and in other hidden places. Borrowers use things that humans have misplaced to help make their homes comfortable. Borrowers were once human size but their fear caused them to become smaller and smaller until they finally became a race of tiny, secretive people. Children may become a part of this fantasy world by creating, in pantomime, a Borrower's home.

As they create the environment in which the Borrowers live, children will gain a deeper understanding of the characters and the story.

PREPARATION: Review books in the Borrowers' series. Arrange book display.

PHYSICAL SETTING: Group sits at one end of the storytelling area. Remainder of the area is left clear for playing.

INTRODUCTION: "Have you ever wondered what happens to things you drop or misplace? It may be possible that the Borrowers have picked them up to use."

Describe Borrowers, their tiny homes and their utter dread of being seen by a human. You might want to read sections of pages 4 and 9 aloud.

PRESENTATION: Show illustrations of Borrowers' home under the floor, pp. 16–7. Discuss how Borrowers used the objects they found. "What other things might the Borrowers find useful?"

"Imagine that this empty space is the home of the Borrowers. Right now there is nothing in it. As Borrowers, you may bring something into the house. Since the object is imaginary, you will have to show what the object is by the way you handle it. Place the object in the house, use it in some way, and then return to your seat. The next person must bring in something different. Watch carefully so you'll remember where and what everything is. If the object is very large or heavy, two Borrowers may place it in the house."

Afterwards discuss what was added to the house and how the Borrowers found it. "Did you have any difficulties moving the objects? Is there anything else you think should be in the Borrowers' home?"

FOLLOW-UP:

1. Introduce the Mary Norton's Borrowers series by Harcout, Brace, Jovanovich.

Norton, Mary. *The Borrowers*. Harcourt, 1953.

———. *The Borrowers Afield*. Harcourt, 1955.

———. *The Borrowers Afloat*. Harcourt, 1959.

———. *The Borrowers Aloft*. Harcourt, 1961.

2. Present other fantasies about small creatures.

Clarke, Pauline. *Return of the Twelves*. Coward, McCann & Geoghegan, 1962.

Kastner, Erich. *The Little Man*. Alfred Knopf, 1966.

Kendall, Carol. *The Gammage Cup*. Harcourt, Brace and World, 1959.

Swift, Jonathan. *Gulliver's Travels*. E. P. Dutton, 1952.

Tolkien, J.R.R. *The Hobbit*. Houghton Mifflin, 1938.

Winterfield, Henry. *Castaways in Lilliput*. Hutchinson, Harcourt, Brace and World, 1960.

VARIATIONS:

1. Use a shoe box and create the Borrower's home with items they might have "borrowed," such as: a thimble, stamp, pencil, etc.

2. Make the Borrowers as spool puppets and use in shoebox-theatre.

3. Create other fantasy creatures as string puppets.

3. Invite children to become Borrowers and use the environment they have just created. "What is one thing you might do before venturing upstairs to borrow something?"

4. Other books to use for creating "the where."

Du Bois, Wm. Pere. *Lion*. Viking, 1956.

Grahame, Kenneth. *Wind in the Willows*. Scribner, 1933.

Lewis, C. S. *The Lion, the Witch, and the Wardrobe*. Macmillan, 1950.

MacDonald, Bettye. *Mrs. Piggle Wiggle*. J. B. Lippincott, 1947.

Tolkien, J. R. R. *The Hobbit*. Houghton Mifflin, 1938.

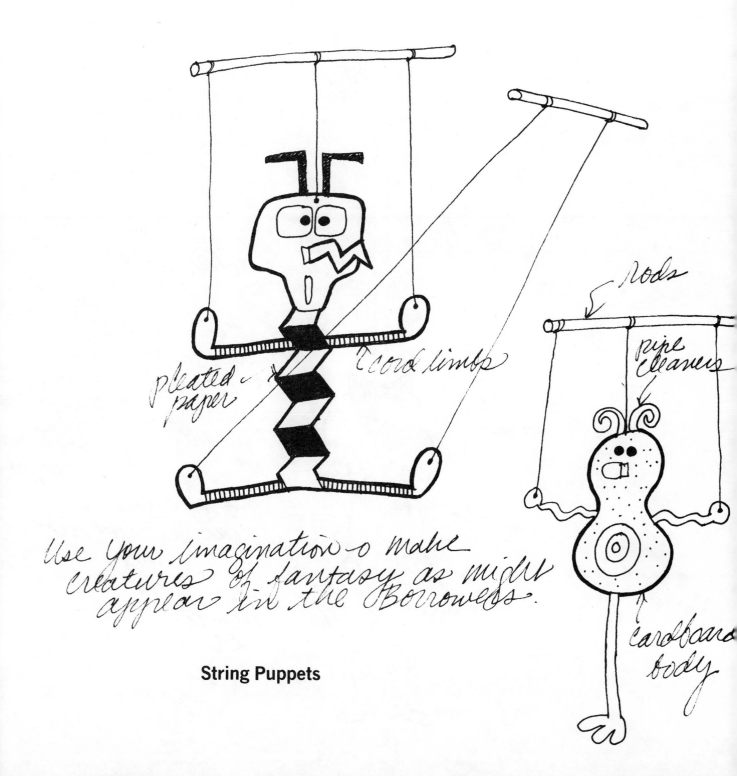

pleated paper

cord limbs

rods

pipe cleaners

cardboard body

Use your imagination o make creatures of fantasy as might appear in the Borrowers.

String Puppets

simple rod puppet

tape plastic
straw rod
on back

stiff paper or
oak tag, cut-out
figure

decorate with
scraps of fabric,
lace and
paper

Shoe Box-Theater

- Create a home for
the Borrowers. Create
furniture from empty
boxes, spools and other
found objects.
- Cut a hole along top of
box to manipulate
simple cut-out figures

107

COSTUME AND SOUND EFFECTS
RESOURCE CENTER

Costume and Sound Effect Resource Center

There is nothing children enjoy more than rummaging through a box of old and colorful costumes, musical instruments and random props. With just a bit of imagination a resource center can easily be set up to help inspire children into role playing with creative dramatics. This could include:

—a hat rack of assorted hats (police, old lady, fire, beach, bride's veil, top hat, etc.)
—a large cardboard box (an appliance box covered with wallpaper) filled with vintage or theatrical costumes (ask about at your local theater groups for left-over costumes.)
—a large cardboard box filled with objects that could be utilized for homemade-improvisational sound effects (such as: blocks of styrofoam found in packaging; kitchen utensils and pots and pans with lids; various size blocks of wood; a metal washing board; etc.)
—a box filled with rhythm instruments (such as castanets, rhythm sticks, drums, wooden blocks, etc.)
—a shelf filled with paper costumes and props.

MOON **HOUND** **BILLY GOAT**

paper strip headband

fabric ears

paper horns

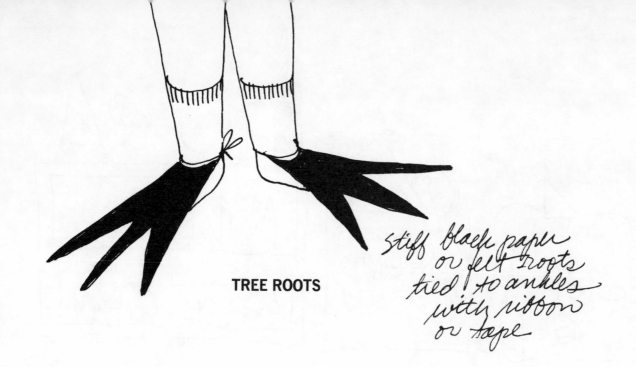

TREE ROOTS

stiff black paper
or felt roots
tied to ankles
with ribbon
or tape

SHEEP   **FOX**   **FLOWER**

large puff of cotton
attached
to
ribbon

fur hat

cardboard shape with
face cutout

pin-on fabric or paper strip tails for animal characters

Head-Band Costumes

curve a 2" wide strip of oak tag or construction paper

use paper clip and adjust width to child's head

BUG   TREE   QUEEN

add antennaes

paper baby birds

sequins.

green fringed tissue paper

SMILE

Paper-Bag Costumes

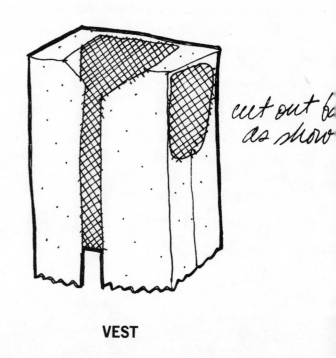

VEST

cut out b..
as show..

For wolf—
1. cut teeth as shown

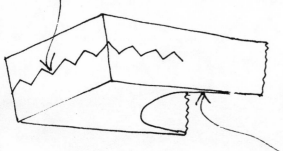

2. cut head-hole at end
3. slip bag over head

WOLF   **BIRD**   **GOLDILOCKS**

4. Staple or tape end close

add paper beak

paint gold curls on bag

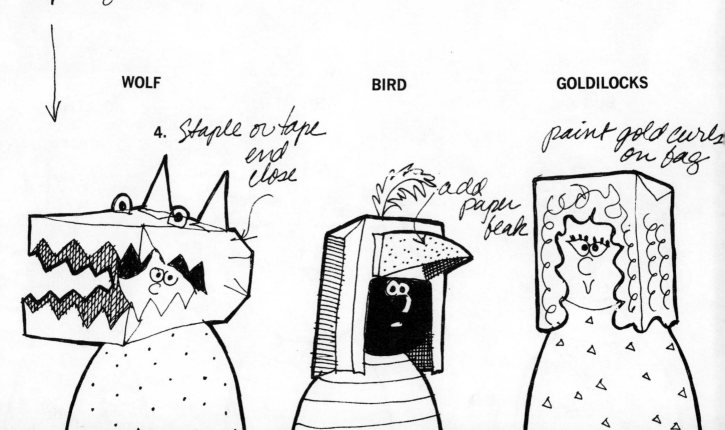

Paper piggy noses and baseball caps comprise the costumes for these three little pigs. Each pig's house is represented by a table, arranged in order of appearance, around the room. Straw, wood blocks and cardboard play-bricks are placed under each table-house. Piggies run from one table-house to another to secure safety underneath, while hiding from the Big Bad Wolf.

Keep in mind, in many creative dramatic activities, to suggest the character in the simpliest and most abstract terms. This allows the imagination to take over to a fuller extent, while minimizing the preparation time in preparing for an activity. Also costumes that are too fussy or cumbersome do not lend themselves well to freedom of movement in expressing dramatic activities.

BIBLIOGRAPHY

PUPPETRY ORGANIZATIONS

PUPPETEERS OF AMERICA—A national organization for the betterment of puppetry, with membership from many parts of the world. An excellent source of inspiration and cohesiveness, it offers: an annual Puppet Festival, held in various parts of the country; the Puppetry Store for purchasing books and puppet items, a bi-monthly magazine; consultant services in all areas of puppetry; and affiliated guilds located in various regions of the country. A small membership fee is required. For information, write to: Puppeteers of America, Gayle G. Schluter, Treasurer, #5 Cricklewood Path, Pasadena, CA 91107.

PUPPETRY IN EDUCATION—A new organization that formed in 1977 because of the growing interest of puppetry in education. Its purpose is to serve as a resource center and puppet store and help unite and share ideas among educators in all areas of puppetry through a monthly newsletter. A small membership fee is required. Write to: Puppetry In Education Project, 164 27th Street, San Francisco CA 94110.

NATIONAL STORYTELLING RESOURCE CENTER—An organization specializing in exploring and upgrading the quality of storytelling techniques. It holds an annual storytelling convention as well as serves as a comprehensive resource center. A special grant is making it possible for this group to compile a unique collection of folk tales. Write to National Storytelling Resource Center, P.O. Box 112, Jonesborough TN 37659.

ONTARIO PUPPETRY ASSOCIATION—A Canadian puppetry organization offering various activities and services. Write to: Kenneth McKay, Executive Secretary, 10 Skyview Crescent, Willowdale, Ontario M2J 1B8, Canada.

BRITISH PUPPET CENTRE—A British group offering various services. Write to: British Puppet Centre, Battersea Town Hall, Lavender Hill, London S.W.11, England.

BRITISH PUPPET AND MODEL THEATRE GUILD—A British group offering various services. Write to: British Puppet and Model Theatre Guild, Mr. G. Shapley, Hon. Secretary, 7 Lupus Street, London SW, England.

THE EDUCATIONAL PUPPETRY ASSOCIATION—A British group involved in using puppetry in education. Write to: Mr. A. R. Philpott, Director, 23A Southampton Place, London WC1A, 2BP, England.

UNIMA ORGANIZATIONS—An international organization with a broad range of activities, including an international annual festival, held at various parts of the world. Write to: *in USA* UNIMA, Mrs. Mollie Falkenstein, General Section of UNIMA, 132 Chiquita Street, Laguna Beach CA 92651; or Mr. Jan Bussell, 16 Riverside, Egham, Surrey, England.

PUPPET MANUFACTURERS

NANCY RENFRO STUDIOS—Offers a most unusual and ambitious selection, including: *show* personalities (people and animals with magnetic appeal!); *educational* types (puppets that teach concepts); *story time characters* (to use with story books); and *loan bag* puppets (over 250 characters to select from, for circulation purposes!) Write to: Nancy Renfro Studios, 1117 W. 9th Street, Austin, TX 78703.

PUPPET MASTERS—A well thought out line of educational media specializing in group puppet-making kits. Write to: Puppet Masters, P.O. Box 11162, Palo Alto, CA 94306.

CLOTH CREATURES—A fun line of fuzzy characters, including a croc-o-gator, Fuzzy Gnome, Small Furry, etc. Write to: Cloth Creatures—Lynne Jennings 281 E. Milan Street, Chula Vista, CA 92010.

POSSUM TROT—Markets an extensive line of cuddly, furry animal characters. Includes woodland creatures such as bunnies and opossums as well as a variety of other animals. Very appealing. Write to: Possum Trot, P.O. Box 249, McKee KY 40447.

MARY MEYERS—Puts out a line of appealing hand puppets in various people characters, with funny noses and personalities. Write to: Mary Meyer Mfg., Townshend VT 05353.

POPPETS—Has available a line of animal characters in a Muppet-like style. Write to: Poppetts, 1800 E. Olive Way, Seattle WA 98102.

ANNIE DEMPSEY—Creates a line of imaginatively crocheted puppets of a more expensive nature, bordering on fantasy. Write to: Annie Dempsey, 4829 Viewmon Street, Holladay UT 94117.

PUPPET FRIENDS—Constructs nicely made, soft and appealing animal and people puppets. Write to: Puppet Friends, 24022 A. Vista Montana, Torrance CA 90505.

PUPPETRY IN EDUCATION—Serves as a resource center for puppetry items and has available puppets, books, and kits. Write to: PIE, 164 27th Street, San Francisco CA 94110.

PUPPET FACTORY—Markets a line of inexpensive, lovable puppet characters, including a knobby-kneed bird, hippy, turtle and other imaginative creatures. Write to Puppet Factory, 160 S. Whisman Road, Mountain View CA 94041.

REEVES INTERNATIONAL, INC.—Distributes high-quality, more expensive line of German made "Steiff" and "Kersa" brand puppets. Write to: Reeves International, Inc., 1107 Broadway, New York NY 10010.

HAPPY HOLLOW PUPPETS, INC.—Creates custom made puppets and scenery to order. Write to: Happy Hollow Puppets, Inc., 324 Zorn Avenue, Louisville KY 40206.

L. K. HECHT CO., INC.—Carries a line of nicely detailed finger puppets. Write to: L. K. Hecht Company, Inc., 1140 Broadway, New York NY 10001.

LESWING PRESS—Sells fairy tale sets in both hand and finger puppets, which include scripts and instructions for play production. Larger puppets are in a Muppet style. Write to: Leswing Press, 750 Adrian Way, San Rafael CA 94903.

PUPPET PRODUCTIONS—Carries an extensive line of colorful, muppet-like people of varied flesh tones. Also a line of funloving animal puppets. This company markets an extensive selection of scripts and cassette tapes geared to Bible and Sunday school themes. Write to: Puppet Productions, P.O. Box 82008, San Diego CA 92138.

DOUGLASS COMPANY, INC.—Markets puppets with "Cat in the Hat" and "Sam I Am" highlights. Write to: Douglass Company, Inc., Keene NH.

PACK-A-LUCK—Markets a line of cute animal and people hand puppets which feature a flexible "sock" talking mouth. Write to: Pack-a-Luck, P.O. Box 18610, Tucson AZ.

GENERAL RESOURCES

Bauer, Caroline. HANDBOOK FOR STORYTELLERS. American Library Association, 1977.

All facets of storytelling are covered: planning; promotion; story sources; multimedia storytelling; and programs. A must for all storytellers.

Cullinan, Bernice E. and *Carolyn W. Carmichael,* eds. LITERATURE AND YOUNG CHILDREN. National Council of Teachers of English, 1977.

A wealth of ideas for sharing literature with young children, especially the preschool child. Includes an annotated list of the "100 Best Books and Authors for Young Children" prepared by the Committee on Literary Experiences for Preschool Children of the National Council of Teachers of English.

Polette, Nancy. E IS FOR EVERYBODY. Scarecrow Press, 1976.

Aptly described by the author as a manual for bringing fine picture books into the hands and hearts of children. An annotation and an activity is in-included for each of the 147 books listed.

Ross, Ramon R. STORYTELLER. Charles E. Merrill, 1975.

A superb book on developing skills in storytelling. Imaginatively and simply presented, this book includes ideas on utilizing songs, puppetry, flannelboard and game exercises to enrich storytelling.

Somers, Albert B. and *Janet Evans Worthington.* RESPONSE GUIDES FOR TEACHING CHILDREN'S BOOKS. National Council of Teachers of English, 1979.

Guides to the twenty-seven books included are designed to spark an enthusiasm for reading as well as reinforcing the teaching of reading skills and interrelating the language arts with other areas of the curriculum. Various activities in art and media, creative dramatics, and composing are included for each book.

Schimmel, Nancy. JUST ENOUGH TO MAKE A STORY. Sisters' Choice Press, 1978.

A small book filled with good advice for storytellers written in a refreshing, personal style. Samples include a fingerplay, cante fable (story with a song in it), and a story accompanied by paperfolding.

PUPPETRY BOOKS

Adair, Margaret Weeks. DO-IT-IN-A DAY PUPPETS FOR BEGINNERS. John Day, 1964.

Instructions and patterns given for a variety of simple puppets. A chapter is devoted to developing the characters of puppets. An easy method for putting puppet stories together using a narrator is described.

Baird, Bill. THE ART OF THE PUPPET. Macmillan, 1965.

Beautiful color photographs highlight this general survey of puppetry. Sure to generate interest and enthusiasm among children of all ages. (PIE)

Cochrane, Louise. SHADOW PUPPETS IN COLOR. Plays, Inc., 1972.

Complete production notes and puppet patterns for three multicultural shadow shows. Upper elementary children will be fascinated as either the puppeteers or the audience.

Puppetry in Education Project. PUPPETRY IN EDUCATION NEWS. (PIE).

The only magazine dedicated entirely to educational puppetry. Articles from educators and puppetry consultants throughout the country include ideas, projects, and experiences. Special interest columns appear in each issue on creativity, libraries, preschool, and curriculum. 6 issues a year for $10. Write to: 164-27th Street, San Francisco, CA 94110.

Renfro, Nancy. PUPPETRY AND THE ART OF STORY CREATION. Nancy Renfro Studios, 1979.

The best description of simple techniques for creating stories and scripts for puppet productions available. The development of creativity is stressed throughout. Many ideas for using puppetry with the hearing impaired child. The second half of this book is filled with unique ideas for creating simple puppets. By the same author *A Puppet Corner in Every Library*.

Renfro, Nancy and *Beverly Armstrong.* MAKE AMAZING PUPPETS. Learn-Works, 1980.

A jammed pack idea-booklet on how to create simple puppets from throwaways and paper products. Imaginative ideas and beautifully illustrated.

Ross, Laura. PUPPET SHOWS USING POEMS AND STORIES. Lothrop, 1970.

A collection of forty-six poems, fables, nursery rhymes, and selections from stories—all equipped with detailed production notes. All are easy to do and require little planning or preparation. By the same author *Hand Puppets: How to Make and Use Them*.

Sims, Judy. PUPPETS FOR DREAMING AND SCHEMING. Early Stages, 1978.

A good introduction for anyone interested in educational puppetry. Ideas for using puppets informally to support curriculum as well as suggestions for producing simple puppet shows. (PIE)

CREATIVE DRAMATICS BOOKS

Carlson, Bernice Wells. PICTURE THAT! Abingdon Press, 1977.

A collection of folktales from around the world. Each story is introduced with a related dramatic activity and followed by an art project. The author also describes how to present these types of activities to children. Also by the same author LET'S PRETEND IT HAPPENED TO YOU.

Cottrell, June. TEACHING WITH CREATIVE DRAMATICS. National Textbook Co., 1975.

An excellent introduction to creative dramatics for anyone working with children. Bibliographies of stories to dramatize with various age groups are included. Storytellers will find the ideas for involving children in stories through sensory and pantomime experiences very useful.

Cullum, Albert. PUSH BACK THE DESKS. Citation Press, 1967.

How Mr. Cullum integrated creative drama principles into his classroom teaching is the subject of this title. Of particular interest to librarians are the chapters dealing with, "Book Blabs," "Poetry Pot," and "Hallway Hoofbeats." Also by the asme author, AESOP IN THE AFTERNOON and SHAKE HANDS WITH SHAKESPEARE.

Heinig, Ruth and *Lydia Stillwell.* CREATIVE DRAMATICS AND THE CLASS-ROOM TEACHER. Prentice Hall, 1974.

A very detailed explanation of creative dramatics techniques. Especially valuable because of the extensive annotated bibliographies of materials suitable for pantomime, dialogue scenes, and story dramatization.

Hennings, Dorothy Grant. SMILES, NODS, AND PAUSES. Citation Press, 1974.

Extensive collection of activities to enrich children's communication skills.

Kraus, Joanna H. SEVEN SOUND AND MOTION STORIES. New Plays for Children, 1971.

Seven sound and action stories that can be used as independent dramatic activities or form the basis of a creative dramatics session. Contains both traditional and modern stories.

Ravosa, Carmino. STORY SONGS. (Record) Omnisound, 1975. $5.95.

Sixteen songs based on favorite stories. Can be used as a basis for pantomime, to introduce characters or a story, and beginning dialogue. A charming record. Available from New Plays for Children, P.O. Box 273, Rowayton, CT, 06853.

Way, Brian. DEVELOPMENT THROUGH DRAMA. Humanities Press, 1967.

A thorough discussion of drama in education. Way stresses the use of drama in the development of the whole child. Of special interest to storytellers are: Chapter 3, "Begin from where you are" which describes how to involve children in sound stories using an arrow for control; and Chapter 4, "Imagination" which discusses how to use stories and sounds to stimulate children's use of their imagination. A *must* for anyone interested in the educational use of drama.